# AMERICA'S LOST TREASURE

# AMERICA'S

A ROUNDTABLE PRESS BOOK

THE ATLANTIC MONTHLY PRESS
NEW YORK

TOMMY THOMPSON

# LOST TREASURE

*Overleaf: The lights of the submersible robot* Nemo
*illuminate the biological and historical mysteries of the deep.*

Copyright © 1998 by Tommy Thompson, with
Columbus-America Discovery Group

Director of Photography: Milt Butterworth, Jr.

A ROUNDTABLE PRESS BOOK
Directors: Marsha Melnick, Susan E. Meyer, Julie Merberg
Project Editor: Rachel D. Carley
Art Director: Richard J. Berenson, Berenson Design & Books, Ltd.
Production Coordinator: John Glenn
Cartography: Bette Duke
Photo Research: Picture Research Consultants, Inc.
Production: Bill Rose

Published simultaneously in Canada
Printed in the United States of America

First Edition

Library of Congress Cataloging-in-Publication Data
Thompson, Tommy, 1952–
     America's lost treasure : a pictorial chronicle of the sinking and
  recovery of the United States mail steamship Central America : the
  ship of gold / Tommy Thompson.
       p.   cm.
     Includes index.
     ISBN 0-87113-732-1
     1. Central America (Ship)—Pictorial works.  2. Shipwrecks—North
  Atlantic Ocean—Pictorial works.  3. Treasure-trove—Pictorial
  works.  4. Survival after airplane accidents, shipwrecks, etc.—
  Pictorial works.   I. Title.
  G530.C4T48  1998
  910′ .91631—dc21                              98–38902
                                                    CIP

2/99

3 1460 00070690 2

THE ATLANTIC MONTHLY PRESS
841 BROADWAY
NEW YORK, NY 10003

98 99 00 01  10 9 8 7 6 5 4 3 2 1

*Gold coins, ingots, and dust*
*are scattered across the*
*degraded timbers.*

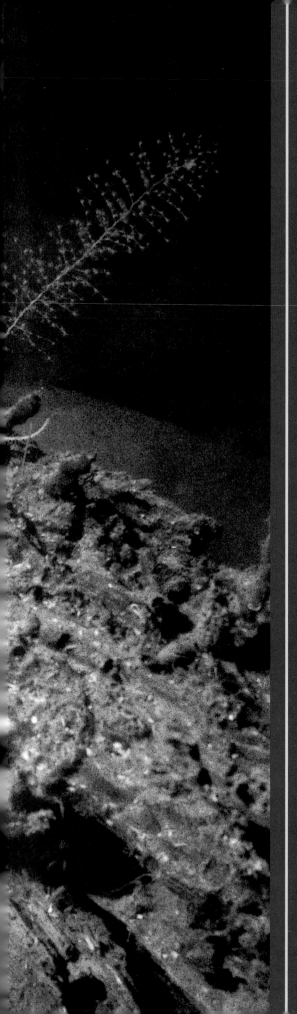

*N*ational treasures—the Crown Jewels of England, King Tut's Tomb, the Amber Room of Russia—are fascinating not only because they are unique, priceless, and of inestimable value, but also because they are symbolic of the cultures that created them. They are more than just collections of precious metals and gems.

# AMERICA'S LOST TREASURE: AN OVERVIEW

Traditional national treasures often represent extravagance and exploitation uncharacteristic of more democratic societies. They often emerge from a strong caste system: a nation's homage to a leader, a king's purposeful accumulation of wealth, an autocrat's share of the labors of his people.

In a democracy like the United States, created "of the people, by the people, for the people," there is no king or pharaoh, no czar, and hence no crowns, no king's jewels, no pharaoh's tombs. Accumulated treasures that do exist in America are either public or private, such as great collections of art or other important cultural relics. However, these tend to lack either the intrinsic monetary value or the national symbolism of traditional national treasures. On rare occasions, a significant treasure may be accumulated accidentally, the result of an act of nature or an act of God.

When the United States Mail Steamship *Central America* sank in deep water off the coast of the Carolinas during a monstrous 1857 hurricane, it created just such an accidental accumulation of treasure. Bound for New York with 578 passengers and crew and 38,000 pieces of mail, the *Central America* also held tons of gold ingots, coins, nuggets, and dust mined from the western gold fields during a defining quarter-century when the country came of age.

Lost for 131 years, the *Central America* shipwreck is a unique time capsule of information and artifacts of an era in which the very character and spirit of America blossomed.

This treasure symbolizes one of the most significant periods in American history, the quarter-century between Samuel Morse's 1837 invention of the telegraph, which launched the country's first electronic information age, and Abraham Lincoln's 1863 Gettysburg Address, which gave voice to the unspoken question that lingered for decades in the hearts and minds of the American people—whether the United States "or any nation so conceived and so dedicated, can long endure."

*Opposite: Gold coins, assay ingots, and nuggets form a time capsule of the mid-19th-century economy.*

In becoming students of this period, we found ourselves part of a movement of people whose interest in American history had increased dramatically. This interest has resulted in a variety of modern perspectives on the quarter-century that included the discovery of western gold, the *Central America*'s sinking, and the economic panic of 1857.

We concur with the school of thinking of noted scholar Page Smith and others who view the period before and after the sinking of the *Central America* as one of the most defining periods in American history, a time when, as Smith titled his 1981 history of the era, "the nation came of age."

The telegraph—the communication miracle of this electronic information age—caused the nation's first electronic information explosion. Until its invention Americans shared news the hard way, by walking, riding a horse, or sailing from one place to another and then returning home. The speed of shared information could be no faster than the speed of any particular round trip.

In the 1840s, as the telegraph became part of the fabric of the nation, Americans east of the Mississippi could share news at the speed of light. News in Savannah reached New York immediately. A presidential address set wires humming throughout the East. Americans began to share their enthusiasms, aspirations, and emotions not only as individuals and regional groups, but also as a nation.

Former New York City mayor Phillip Hone said of this particular time: "Newspapers have become the most agreeable of all reading, so exciting and so colorful are the movements and events of the age. By the magic aid of . . . Morse's telegraph . . . everything that occurs of the slightest importance is almost instantly known."

The dramatic increase in the speed of shared information led to a dramatic increase in "emotional connectedness." With the ability to exchange ideas quickly, being an American became a more immediately shared experience. For the first time, many Americans began to believe in their hearts and minds that the democratic experiment was succeeding and prospering. That belief allowed the national character to blossom into a uniquely American spirit and a robust drive toward progress. The American dream was alive.

In 1893, noted scholar Frederick Jackson Turner defined this developing American character as a "coarseness and strength combined with acuteness and acquisitiveness; that practical inventive turn of mind, quick to find expedients, that masterful grasp of material things; that restless, nervous energy; that dominant individualism."

Almost a century after Turner, Americans are still strong, inventive, and individualistic, characteristics that have carried the nation to the forefront of the world stage.

Today many nations around the world admire and emulate what it means to be American. Americans, both as individuals and as a nation, are characterized as spirited, optimistic, visionary, forward-thinking, adaptable, and entrepreneurial, traits symbolized by the pioneers, adventurers, and nation-builders aboard the *Central America*.

With courage and ingenuity, passengers and crew endured the hurricane and bailed their sinking ship for more than 40 hours. In a final heroic act, Captain William Lewis Herndon and his crew rescued the women and children by lowering them into lifeboats at the sacrifice of their own lives. The values and beliefs that inspired their industry in life and tenacity in the face of death endure today in a shared American spirit.

**\* \* \***

Through text and images we present *America's Lost Treasure: A Pictorial Chronicle of the Sinking and Recovery of the United States Mail Steamship* Central America—*The Ship of Gold*. We invite you to explore this defining period, to understand this treasure, and to place it within its historical and cultural context.

**\* \* \***

## Regarding National Treasures

Over the past 35 years, academic institutions, governments, and United Nations conferences have worked to define "treasures of national heritage." The international legal community and individual policy makers and scholars have contributed to the growing dialogue.

While formal criteria for defining *national treasure* have not been universally adopted, they tend toward the symbolic, relating the treasure's cultural and historical significance to the nation as a whole.

Based on the recurring themes that scholars use to compare, contrast, and evaluate national treasures, we concur that any national treasure can be evaluated by certain defining characteristics.

Worldwide, most (but not all) national treasures tend to possess the following qualities:

• Symbolic value—being symbolic of a nation itself

• Extraordinary intrinsic and monetary value

• Unique and irreplaceable to the nation

• Cultural value—being representative of a significant part of the
 core culture of the nation

• Work of human hands as a form of cultural expression of the nation

• Historical significance—tied to important historical events of the nation

• Inherent aesthetic value

It would be unusual for a national treasure created in a democratic society to possess every one of these qualities. Coincidentally, the treasure of the *Central America* possesses all these qualities.

## Documenting the Treasure of the *Central America*

From the outset we sought to recover the *Central America* because years of research documented that it possessed extraordinary symbolic, cultural, and intrinsic monetary value. It provides our nation and its people the opportunity to establish stewardship of a treasure of national heritage and what it symbolizes.

The extensive film and video documentation and careful recovery and preservation of passenger and ship artifacts present a rare chance to understand more about this defining period in which the American spirit and national character blossomed. The gold, the historic artifacts, and the scientific information, in a sense, belong to the American people. The rescue of this treasure from the deep ocean has returned it to all of us.

We believe this treasure and what it symbolizes should be recognized and honored in such a way as to preserve it for future generations. Now it must weather the storms of time, commerce, and competing interests to endure as a symbol of the American dream and the American spirit.

Thomas G. Thompson, Founder
Columbus-America Discovery Group
Columbus, Ohio
1998

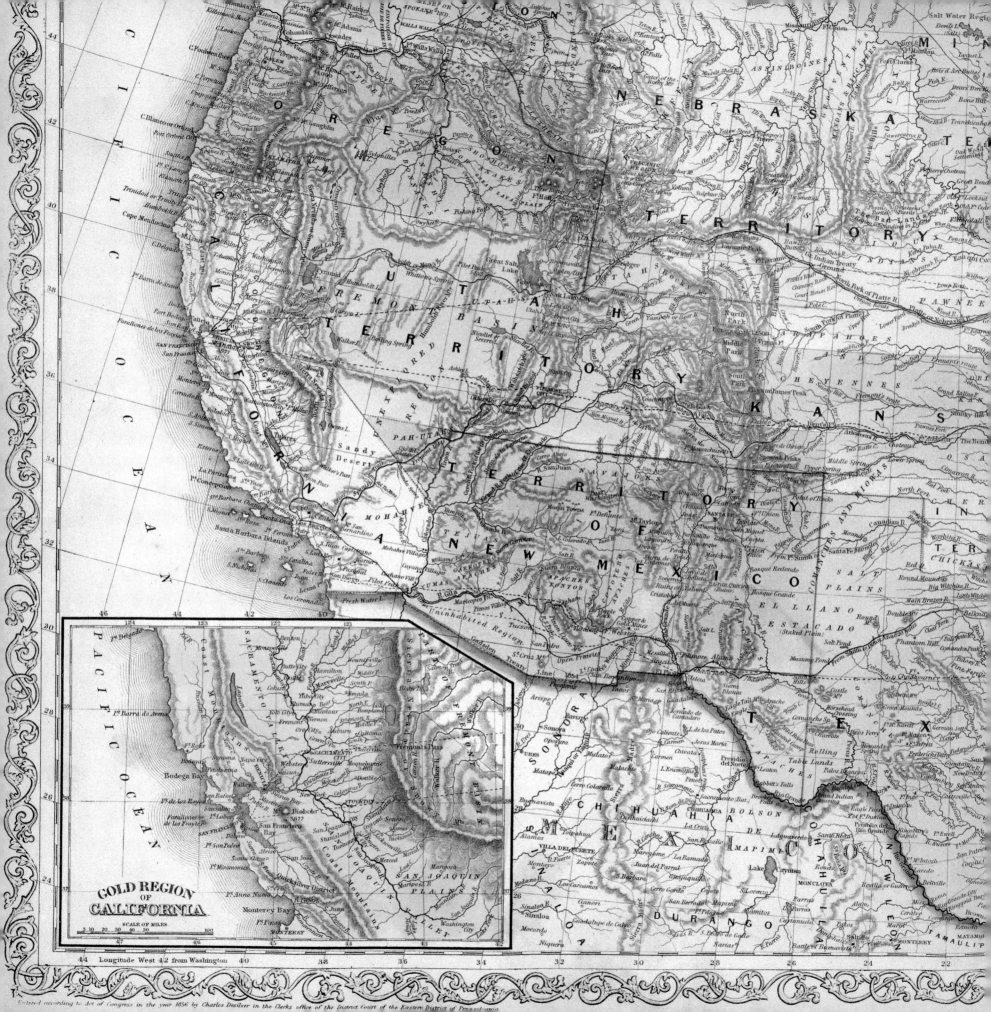

GOLD REGION
OF
CALIFORNIA

SCALE OF MILES
5 10 20 30 40 50    100

Longitude West 42 from Washington

Entered according to Act of Congress in the year 1856 by Charles Desilver in the Clerks office of the District Court of the Eastern District of Pennsylvania

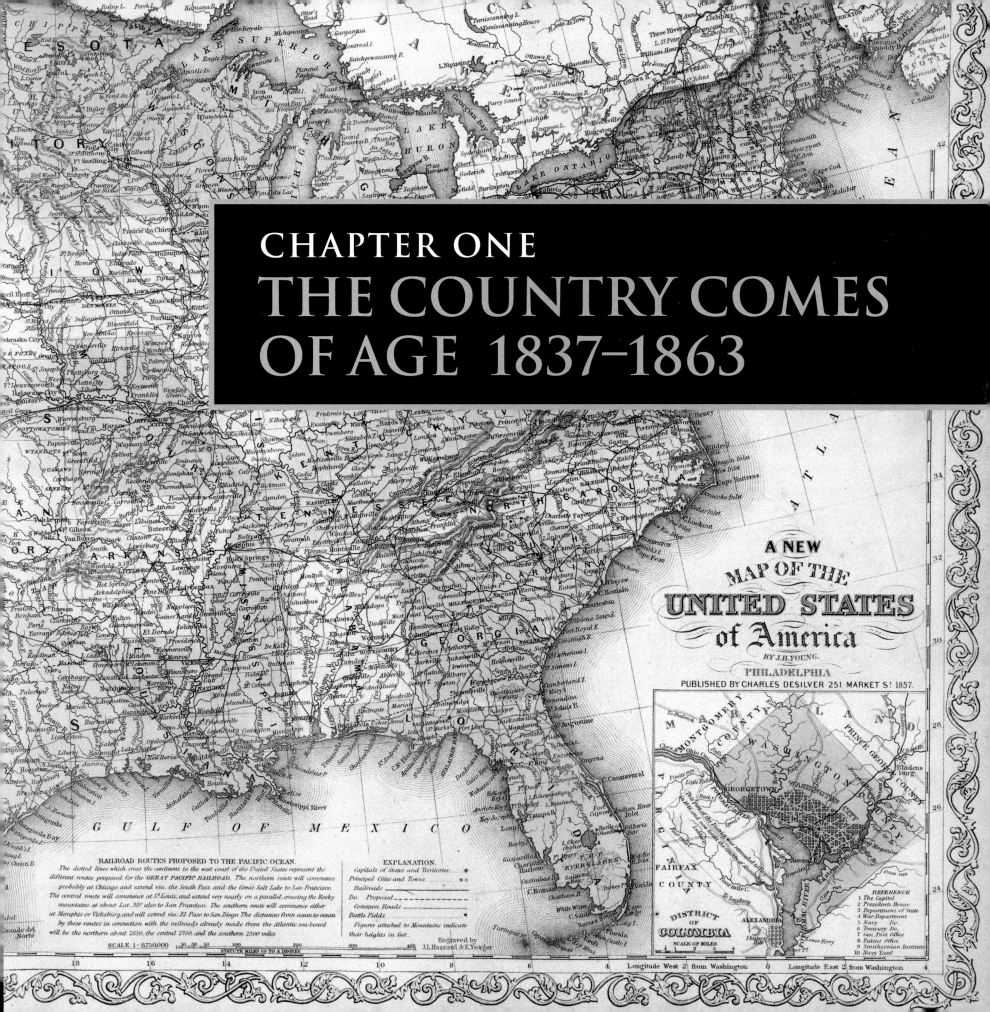

CHAPTER ONE

# THE COUNTRY COMES OF AGE 1837–1863

On August 20, 1857, more than 400 passengers boarded a sidewheel steamship at the Vallejo Street Wharf in San Francisco. They were bound for New York on a combined sea-and-land journey via the Panama Route: steamship down the Pacific Coast to Panama, a brief train ride over the isthmus, and a second sidewheeler to New York. When that second ship, the elegant United States Mail Steamship *Central America,* left Panama on September 3 for the final leg up the Atlantic coast, it carried a fairly typical cargo, including 38,000 pieces of mail. Also on board: tons of California gold, including several commercial shipments, as well as the ingots, coins, nuggets, and dust carried by passengers.

The *Central America* never reached its destination. On September 9, one day out of a port call in Havana, the three-masted sidewheeler ran into a monstrous hurricane and, after gallantly fighting the storm for three days, finally sank somewhere far off the Carolinas. Its spectacular treasure disappeared thousands of feet into the cold, lightless depths, impossibly far from the reach of man. Although there were 153 survivors, 425 people died in what remains the worst peacetime ocean disaster in United States history.

Nearly a century and a half later, the *Central America* and its treasure are not merely part of a haunting legend of tragedy but the vivid symbol of an era of unprecedented expansion through exploration, travel, and commerce. The passenger list alone—composed of lawyers and wage earners, merchants and gamblers, miners and immigrants, entrepreneurs and young families—was a revealing cross-section of an increasingly diverse mid-19th-century population.

Moreover, the ship itself represents the great advances in communications and technology that helped define the formative period when the nation was coming of age: the years between Samuel Morse's invention of the telegraph in 1837 and Abraham Lincoln's 1863 Gettsyburg Address. In the 1830s and 1840s, steamships like the *Central America* were replacing wind-dependent sailing ships on the high seas as the best and fastest means of travel and source

*Overleaf: A map drawn by J. H. Young and published in 1857 by Charles DeSilver of Philadelphia shows the United States and territories at that time.*

of news. A major transportation advance, the sidewheelers traveling the Panama Route also carried mail and thus served as an important link between different regions of the rapidly expanding country. That connection was strengthened by another 19th-century innovation: the telegraph, which sent information over thousands of miles of wire far faster than it could be transported by steamship.

*On August 20, 1857, the steamship* Sonora *left San Francisco on its first leg of the Panama Route. In Panama, the passengers and a fortune in California gold were transferred to the* Central America *for the journey to New York. Pictured here in an 1862 photograph, the* Sonora *is departing San Francisco for the trip down the Pacific Coast—exactly as it had done that warm summer day five years earlier.*

As travel and communication improved in this period, industry boomed, bolstered by Machine Age advancements ranging from the cotton gin to the sewing machine to vulcanized rubber. While eastern cities grew, however, the West remained a harsh and sparsely settled territory prior to the gold rush of 1849. Of the total U.S. population of 20 million in 1845, fewer than 1.5 million lived beyond the Mississippi. The great majority of those settled just west of the river in Arkansas and Missouri. On the vast and nearly empty plains, homesteaders scratched out a meager and often dangerous existence. Staples and commercial goods were scarce, and luxuries nonexistent.

## CALIFORNIAN.

SAN FRANCISCO, WEDNESDAY, MARCH 15, 1849.

GOLD MINE FOUND.—In the newly made raceway of the Saw Mill recently erected by Captain Sutter, on the American Fork, gold has been found in considerable quantities. One person brought thirty dollars worth to New Helvetia, gathered there in a short time. California, no doubt, is rich in mineral wealth; great chances here for scientific capitalists. Gold has been found in almost every part of the country.

*On March 15, 1849, the* San Francisco Californian *scooped the world on one of the greatest news stories in American history: the discovery of gold in California.*

Because the telegraph did not yet stretch beyond the Mississippi, the steamship remained the most efficient communication and travel link to the far western edge of the continent, where life was hard and the sense of isolation extreme. Indeed, in the mid-1840s, California was little more than a collection of dusty missions and dirt trails with fewer than 15,000 hardy settlers.

Trade outposts such as Yerba Buena, which sat on a picturesque bay in the north, were just clusters of fewer than 500 pioneers. Change, however, was imminent. In 1847, Yerba Buena became San Francisco, and the federal government brought California under U.S. military control. The fate of the region turned abruptly in January of the following year with a chance discovery by a young carpenter named James Marshall. Inspecting the progress of work on a sawmill he was building on the American River with his partner, John Sutter, Marshall found gold.

"My eye was caught by something shining in the bottom of the ditch," he said later. "I reached my hand down and picked it up; it made my heart thump, for I was certain it was gold. . . . Then I saw another." Marshall and Sutter tried to keep their find a secret, but the news made its way into small newspapers such as the *California Star* and traveled widely up and down the bay. By mid-June, settlers and visitors alike were leaving outposts like San Francisco nearly empty. Setting up campsites along the rivers near what is now Sacramento and

in the canyons and gulches of the Sierra Nevada foothills, they would pan for gold from sunup to sundown.

Later that summer of 1848, Colonel Richard B. Mason, the military governor of the California Territory, toured the region accompanied by his chief of staff, Lieutenant William Tecumseh Sherman. The two estimated that some 4,000 men were working what were commonly known as "the gold fields," daily extracting $30,000 to $50,000 worth of the precious metal, "if not more." The colonel's report went to Washington, D.C., along with $3,900 worth of nuggets and dust.

*James Wilson Marshall, shown at Sutter's Mill in 1853, discovered gold there in 1848. Though his discovery made thousands of other people wealthy—and ultimately changed the world—Marshall himself died in poverty.*

*Overleaf: This painting by Victor Prevost shows Yerba Buena in 1847, the year the port city was renamed San Francisco. At that time the sleepy settlement had a population of fewer than 500 people. By the end of 1849, however, the influx of gold seekers had swelled its numbers to 25,000 spirited, rowdy, and often contentious souls.*

19

*This determined Forty-Niner is carrying everything the well-equipped miner could conceivably need, from gold pan to cooking pot to firearms.*

Six months later, on December 5, Mason's report was the highlight of President James K. Polk's opening message to the Second Session of the Thirtieth Congress. "The accounts of the abundance of gold in that territory are of such an extraordinary character as would scarcely command belief were they not corroborated by authentic reports," the president declared. The nation's newspapers immediately seized on the story, igniting enthusiasm among the populace and spurring each other on to greater heights of editorial fervor. Gold fever became a national—and even international—epidemic as tens of thousands raced to the Sacramento Valley from around the country as well as from South America, Asia, and Europe.

"The spirit of emigration which is carrying off thousands to California . . . increases and expands every day," reported the *New York Herald* on January 11, 1849, less than a year after Marshall's discovery. "All classes of our citizens seem to be under the influence of this extraordinary mania. . . . Poets, philosophers, lawyers, brokers, bankers, merchants, farmers, clergy men—all are feeling the impulse and are preparing to go and dig for gold and swell the number of adventurers to the new El Dorado." Singing new tunes like "Oh, Susannah," the anthem of the gold rush, the Forty-Niners were exuberant, giddy with dreams. Their boundless optimism was further stoked by waves of new literature such as *The Emigrant's Guide to the Gold Mines*, one of many hot-selling but highly fanciful "guidebooks" that told of "rivers paved with gold to the thickness of a hand."

Many believed that all one had to do to claim a fortune in California was to reach into a cold mountain stream and pick up a handful of gold. Once in the gold fields, however, most discovered that the work produced more exhaustion and disappointment than gold, and they found themselves in need of two companions: labor and luck.

Disillusioned veterans told tales of backbreaking work, aching loneliness, and nothing to show for it at the end. Still the dreamers came. All that seemed to

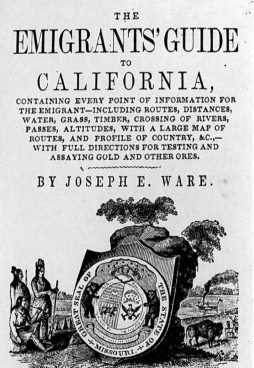

*Left: Gold fever infects the Long Island post office that is the subject of this 1850 painting by William Mount.*

*Below: The gold rush inspired many largely fanciful guidebooks to the gold fields. This offering was among the most practical of the lot, but its author had never been to California. When he finally attempted the overland journey, he died of cholera.*

THE
# EMIGRANTS' GUIDE
TO
## CALIFORNIA,
CONTAINING EVERY POINT OF INFORMATION FOR
THE EMIGRANT—INCLUDING ROUTES, DISTANCES,
WATER, GRASS, TIMBER, CROSSING OF RIVERS,
PASSES, ALTITUDES, WITH A LARGE MAP OF
ROUTES, AND PROFILE OF COUNTRY, &C.,—
WITH FULL DIRECTIONS FOR TESTING AND
ASSAYING GOLD AND OTHER ORES.

BY JOSEPH E. WARE.

PUBLISHED BY J. HALSALL,
No. 124 MAIN STREET,
ST. LOUIS, MO.

matter was the chance to make a fortune overnight. That, and the sheer adventure of it all. Not all frontier entrepreneurs sought their fortunes in gold. Many stayed in San Francisco, choosing the greater security of selling supplies and services. Saloons, bordellos, and minstrel shows generated a raucous energy that early on characterized this boomtown of mostly male, transient adventurers. Shops opened and the muddy streets rang with the cacophonous shouts of merchants hawking pans, knives, buckets, tents, and blankets.

With the clattering wagons and strained voices—the sounds of urgency, commerce, and rampant individualism—early San Francisco was a decidedly raw and rough-hewn settlement where anything could happen. Hustlers who had been snake-oil salesmen elsewhere found they could market ingenious, if often

# Routes to the Gold Fields

Travelers wishing to go from the East Coast to the West Coast or back again during the gold rush of the 1850s had three choices: crossing the country by one of several overland trails; sailing "around the Horn;" or taking a sea-and-land voyage by way of either the "Panama Route" or the "Nicaraguan Route," depending on which isthmus was crossed during the journey.

The overland route was the shortest and most direct of the three, and usually the cheapest. However, as it took from four to six months to complete and involved walking much of the way beside a covered wagon, this was certainly the most physically exhausting way to travel. Accidents and illnesses also took a toll.

As a result, many people traveling between the two coasts chose the alternate Cape Horn route around the tip of South America—about 13,000 miles by sail from New York to San Francisco. The fastest Cape Horn voyage during the gold rush era—88 days—was made by the clipper ship *Flying Cloud*. Although cheaper than the Panama Route, the trip would typically take four to six months or even longer, depending on the winds. One particular voyage described in the ship's log lasted nine long and dreadful months as the ship lay becalmed for many weeks at a time at several points along its route.

Those who could afford it preferred the quicker but more expensive Panama Route, which eliminated the long leg around Cape Horn. Travelers from San Francisco to New York took a steamship south 3,000 miles down the Pacific Coast to Panama and crossed the isthmus overland. Once on the other side, they boarded a second steamship at the Caribbean port of Aspinwall (now Colón) for the 2,000-mile leg to New York, with one port of call in Havana. The entire passage, also offered in reverse, usually took 19 to 24 days.

Before 1855, when the Panama Railroad was completed, the isthmian crossing was probably the most

The arrivals and departures of Panama Route steamers from San Francisco were exciting occasions, with friends waving each other good-bye. The twice-monthly steamships were vital to Californians, who depended on them for commerce and communication with the rest of the country.

make their own way by dugout canoe and on muleback through the steamy, fever-ridden jungle, a trip that could take five days or more. The Panama Railroad reduced this hazardous trek to a relatively pleasant four-hour excursion. Passengers disembarking on one side of the isthmus in the morning at Panama City could count on being at sea aboard the second steamship on the Caribbean side that same afternoon.

While the sidewheelers were reasonably comfortable, three weeks at sea was still enough time to make the trip monotonous. Passengers also faced exposure to deadly tropical diseases such as dysentery, yellow fever, and cholera in both Panama and Havana. Nevertheless, the Panama Route was by far the safest and most agreeable means of travel from coast to coast. During the two decades between 1848 and 1869, about 640,000 passengers traveled this route, also used to carry U.S. mail.

There was precious cargo, as well. The *Central America* made 43 round trips between New York and Panama, carrying nearly a third of the gold transported from California to New York between 1853 and

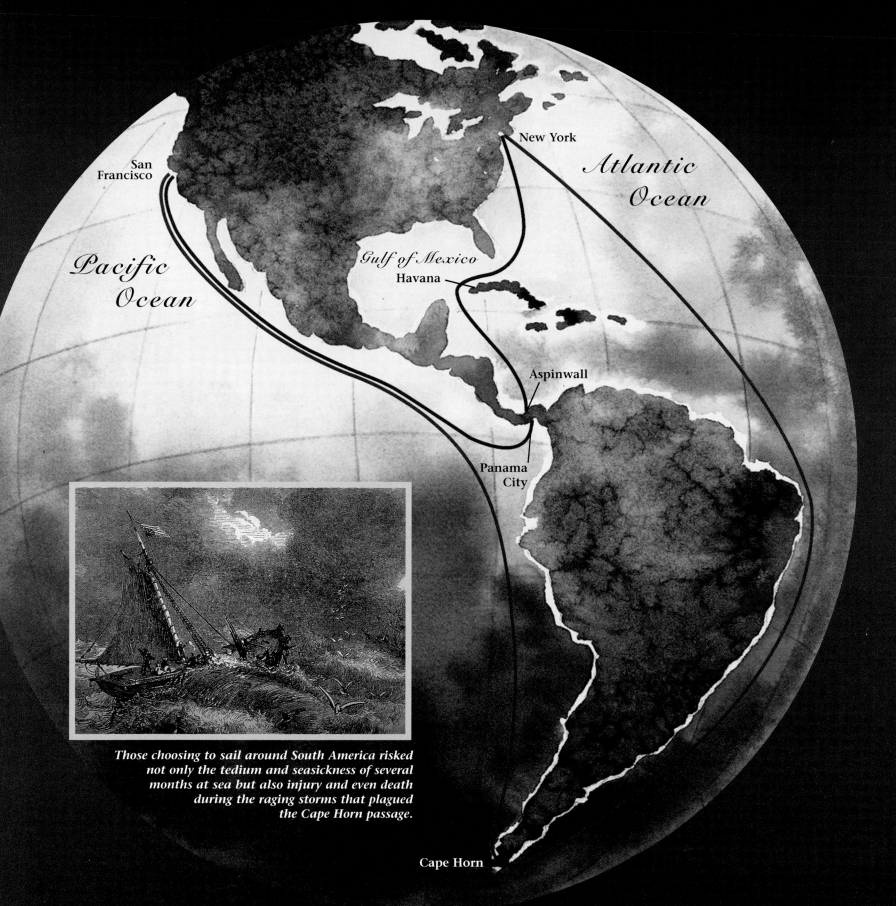

San
Francisco

*Pacific
Ocean*

*Gulf of Mexico*

Havana

New York

*Atlantic
Ocean*

Aspinwall

Panama
City

Cape Horn

*Those choosing to sail around South America risked
not only the tedium and seasickness of several
months at sea but also injury and even death
during the raging storms that plagued
the Cape Horn passage.*

25

*Contrary to rumor, the streets of San Francisco were not paved with gold. In fact, in the early years, they were not paved with anything at all, as this illustration by English artist Frank Marryat shows.*

useless, mining devices. Legitimate businessmen, such as Levi Strauss, inventor of blue jeans, got started there during this era, as well.

By 1849, a mere 18 months after it had numbered just a few hundred souls, San Francisco had jumped to 25,000 gold-hungry citizens, and by 1855 the population had soared to 55,000. In 1850, just a year into the rush, the population of California had grown from 18,000 to 92,600 and the territory was made the 31st state. The emerging metropolis, with increasing wealth, luxuries from the East,

*The rapid growth of San Francisco's population caused severe lumber shortages. However, because many sailors deserted to seek their fortunes in the gold fields, abandoned sailing ships were plentiful and were sometimes hauled on shore and set up as "storeships."*

*Above: In this 1850 painting by J. R. Eyerman, California miners separate gold dust, flakes, and nuggets from gravel with a "long tom."*

*Left: A prospector uses the traditional, and more affordable, method of panning.*

# Mining the Gold

Despite James Marshall's discovery of a large nugget in the American River and the vivid descriptions in guidebooks that followed—proclaiming gold-lined streams in the foothills of the Sierras—most Forty-Niners found the work of mining the gold more arduous than whatever occupation they had left behind. Separated from their families, they camped alongside rivers for months at a time, either alone or in groups, and were exposed mercilessly to the elements.

The miner's basic tool was a shallow pan, in which water would be washed continually over sediment until any gold, which was eight times heavier than stones or sand, would be left in the bottom.

As the day wore on, the miner's legs and hands would grow numb from the icy water, while his entire body ached. As a result, labor-saving variations on the pan appeared. These included the cradle, a device that was rocked as sediment was poured into the top and then panned out the bottom. Another innovation was the sluice, a long trough with bars, or "riffles," on the bottom, which caught gold from the constantly cascading water and sediment. Based on a similar principle, the "long tom" was a trough designed to filter sediment through a "riddle" before directing it to a "riffle box" that separated the gold.

29

*Above: In mid-1849, more than 500
sailing ships lay abandoned in San
Francisco harbor. Their crews had
deserted to seek their fortunes in this
new promised land.*

and growing numbers of South Americans, Europeans, and Chinese, was increasingly heterogeneous. A less transient, upper class of merchants, bankers, and socially prominent citizens also developed. By the mid-1850s the prosperous new state of California was sending millions of dollars in gold to the East via the Panama Route.

The gold was important not only for its economic value but also as a magnet that lured hundreds of thousands of Americans west. That, in turn, says historian Page Smith in his 1981 book *The Nation Comes of Age*, helped shape a large national consciousness, for "more important than the several hundred thousand Americans who made the desperately arduous journey to the gold fields . . . was the fact that the American imagination was 'enlarged' by the rush to reach out to the shores of the Pacific and comprehend the continent."

Less than a decade later, in the midst of the Civil War, President Lincoln would mark the end of this important period of development with his 1863

MERCHANTS' EXPRESS LINE OF CLIPPER SHIPS FOR SAN FRANCISCO.
Passages 106 & 117 Days.

THE WELL-KNOWN     EXTREME CLIPPER SHIP

# EAGLE WING

LINNELL, Commander, is now loading at Pier 16 E. R.

For Freight, apply at once to

**RANDOLPH M. COOLEY**, 88 Wall St., Tontine Building.

Agents in San Francisco, Messrs. DE WITT, KITTLE & CO.

NESBITT & CO., PRINTERS, N. Y.

*Left: Clipper ships could make the trip around the Horn to California fairly rapidly, as illustrated by this advertisement for projected passages of 106 and 117 days. The quickest trip ever made by a clipper ship, the Flying Cloud, was 88 days. However, even these, the fastest sailing ships, couldn't come close to the time made by steamers on the Panama Route: 19 to 24 days.*

# Harnessing the Lightning

*A*rticle I, Section 8 of the United States Constitution contains a simple provision: "To establish Post Offices and Post Roads." It was also an essential one. When the Constitution was framed in the 18th century, communication required travel, and relatively few Americans were able to travel very far from home. This was still true in the early 1800s, when post offices were among the most important connections between village and city and information and ideas moved at the speed of ships and horses. If the weather was good and the roads were dry, a resident of Philadelphia could expect news from Boston that was only four or five days old. However, news could take months to cross the country, and frontier settlements heard about events in distant regions long after the fact.

The first major breakthrough in communication

*Telegraph-station patrons handwrote messages, which a clerk then wired in Morse code.*

*Samuel Morse's telegraph key was used to send the first trial message.*

came in 1837, when Samuel F. B. Morse invented the telegraph. By "harnessing the lightning," Morse ushered in America's first electronic information explosion with his code of short and long electrical impulses, and the telegraph became the miracle of the age.

By the 1840s, telegraph lines spread throughout the country east of the Mississippi. Although expanding westward faster than the wires could, the nation was still connected better than ever before. In many more areas, ideas and news could be shared almost instantly. As telegraph operators in Boston fired out a rapid code of dots and dashes over the lines, people in Chicago, Richmond, and New Orleans could know the news in minutes. National reaction to events became much more immediate as viewpoints of newspaper editors around the country were compared and contrasted. The country could "feel its nationhood."

*Left: A miner has his gold weighed in the Wells Fargo office.*

*Below: An ingot bears the mark of Blake & Co., a Sacramento assayer.*

Gettysburg Address, in which he spoke of rededicating efforts to the task of preserving the American form of government after the war. In many ways, the nation had completed its expansion from East Coast to West, and now it was time to reassess the identity of the Union.

The travelers aboard the *Central America* were pioneers of this passing era. Most had followed their imaginations west and hence were among the first to "comprehend the continent." When they set sail for New York City on September 3, 1857, they thought themselves to be safely aboard one of the wonders of the age. For all their imagination, however, they could never have supposed that the United States Mail Steamship *Central America* and the treasure aboard would become the stuff of speculation and legend for more than 130 years.

# "The Confusion and Panic of the Day"

uring the national expansion of the 1850s, gold flowed from the West Coast to the East in biweekly shipments, while railroads and riverboats pushed from the East Coast into the West, making it easier for farmers to get their grain to markets. Grain exports doubled, and much of the California gold was also exported to keep its price from falling. As gold output increased, however, its value fell, and prices of almost everything else rose.

By early 1857, the storm clouds of recession had gathered. Overseas demand for American wheat declined just as imports began to hurt the American textile industry. At the same time, speculation in domestic cotton and railroads reached new heights. Led by agriculture, individual sectors of the economy began to draw against their bank deposits, putting greater and greater pressure on the gold

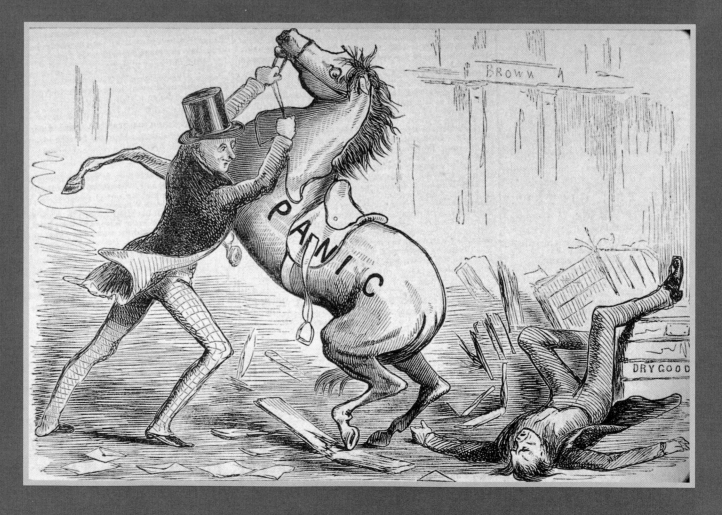

*In this illustration from* Harper's Weekly, *the Panic of 1857 is portrayed as a runaway horse threatening the populace.*

34

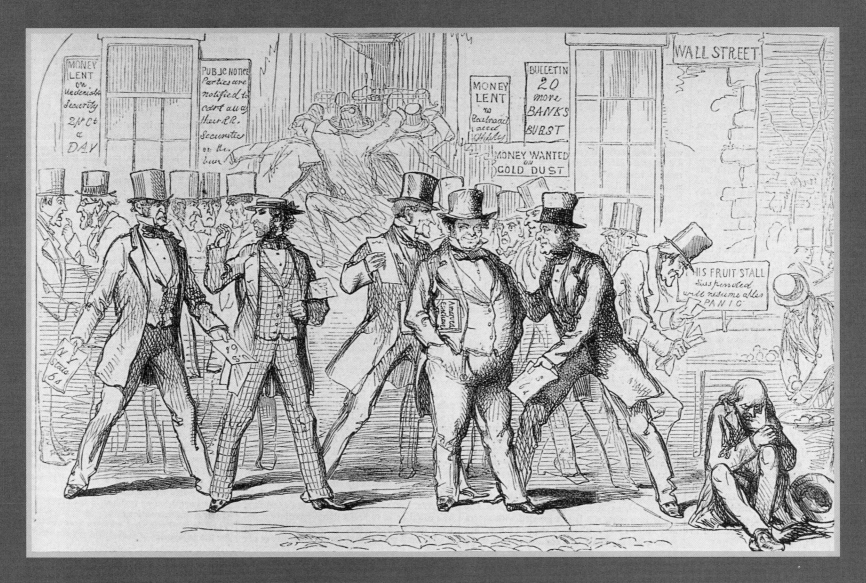

reserves that banks relied upon to back their privately issued notes.

In August 1857, the bubble burst. The New York office of the Ohio Life Insurance and Trust Company closed its doors. Most New York banks were creditors of Ohio Life, and, as prices fell and the values vanished, several of those banking firms failed. A concurrent delay of gold shipments from California contributed to the despair. This was compounded by the sinking of the *Central America*, which sent its huge load of gold—historian Bray Hammond estimates a value equal to one-fifth of the gold then in Wall Street coffers—to the bottom of the sea.

With that gold, it had been hoped that banks could withstand any run; without it they were at grave risk of failure. General William Tecumseh Sherman, a New York banker at the time of the sinking, wrote in his memoirs that the "absolute loss of this treasure went to swell the confusion and panic of the day."

*Some speculators profited from the Panic—like the smug fellow pictured at the center of this* Harper's Weekly *illustration. Many others, however, lost everything, as illustrated by the poor soul at right.*

# CHAPTER TWO
# LAST VOYAGE

"Steamer day" in San Francisco—the day of departure or arrival of one of the biweekly Panama Route steamships—was always a lively occasion, with bands playing, flags flying, and enthusiastic crowds seeing off departing friends or greeting new arrivals. The morning of Thursday, August 20, 1857, was no exception, as more than 400 eastbound passengers and their friends and well-wishers excitedly crowded the Vallejo Street Wharf. At the dock was the SS *Sonora*, the ship that would take the passengers on the first leg of their journey to New York.

It was a colorful group, representing every level of San Francisco society. First-cabin passengers included Billy Birch, the 26-year-old star of the famous San Francisco Minstrels, and his vivacious wife, Virginia. The young couple had exchanged wedding vows the day before. Another honeymooning couple, Adeline and Ansel Easton, arrived at the wharf directly from their morning wedding, escorted by an entourage of high-society friends. Addie was the sister of the banker Darius Ogden Mills, who later co-founded the Bank of California and became one of the richest men in the state.

*Ansel Ives Easton
and Adeline Mills
Easton were
honeymooners
traveling on the
Central America.
Adeline's later
correspondence
indicates the couple
were very much in love.*

There were other prominent San Francisco residents making the voyage, as well. Rufus Allen Lockwood and his wife, Harriet, were there, accompanied by three of their five children. Lockwood had a reputation as one of the finest lawyers in California and also as something of an eccentric. The attorney habitually disappeared from his family and law office for months at a time; most recently he had spent a year away from home in Australia herding sheep.

Other passengers, less prosperous (or perhaps more thrifty) had purchased steerage tickets. Among them were 17-year-old Henry T. O'Connor, a printer, and his widowed mother.

The Sonora, *launched in 1854, was a wooden two-masted steamer built by J. A. Westervelt and Company.*

George Dawson, a free African American who had been working as a hotel porter, was also heading east. Oliver Perry Manlove, a veteran of three adventurous years in the gold fields at the young age of 26, was making his first journey by sea; in 1854 he had come west overland by covered wagon. With him, Manlove carried a sheaf of poems he had written describing his adventures.

The fare for any type of cabin was not cheap. In 1857, a first-cabin ticket on the Panama Route cost $300 and a second-cabin ticket $250. Steerage accommodations sold for $150, which was the equivalent of a month's wages for the average California gold prospector, who made about $5 a day.

Thus, even those in steerage class had money, and in 1857—especially in gold rush–era California—money meant gold. "Many were persons of large means," an 1857 issue of the *Chicago Tribune* later reported of the travelers, "and there

*Above: Edward W. Hull, the Central America's purser, was one of the unsung heroes of the disaster. He stuck to his post, refusing to leave the sinking ship until all the passengers were saved.*

*Below: Edward's brother, William H. Hull, the storekeeper, was equally brave. Both men died in the disaster.*

*Above: Dr. Alvin Ellis and his wife, Lynthia, were returning home to Ohio with four children. Dr. Ellis died, but Mrs. Ellis and the children were saved by the* Marine.

*Right: First-cabin passenger William (Billy) Birch, a nationally famous minstrel comedian, was traveling with his new bride, Virginia. Billy was rescued by the* Ellen *and Virginia by the* Marine.

*Left: Amanda Marvin, a brave and energetic young woman from Chicago who was traveling with her husband, William, volunteered to help bail water. She is shown dressed in men's clothes, because, as she explained, "I thought if I had them on they would let me work, and think I was a boy." Believing that bailing was their work, however, the men were too gallant to allow it. Amanda was rescued by the Marine, but her husband was lost.*

*Above: Rufus Allen Lockwood, a brilliant but eccentric San Francisco attorney, had been given to mysterious disappearances throughout his life. He died on the Central America, and his wife, Harriet, returned home to Lafayette, Indiana, with the children. Harriet survived the loss of the ship by 40 years but reportedly had become so accustomed to Lockwood's frequent disappearances that she fully expected him to one day reappear.*

*Above: A typical first-cabin stateroom on a Panama steamer usually contained three berths, one above another.*

*"The floors were covered with carpet, and the berths were screened with outer damask curtains, extending from top to bottom, and inner cambric curtains."*
— *John Haskell Kemble*

*Right: So many washbowls, water pitchers, and soap dishes were found on the shipwreck site that researchers believe they were standard cabin equipment.*

were but very few whose immediate wealth did not amount to hundreds, while numbers reckoned their gold by the thousands of dollars." Tons of the precious metal made up the shipments on the Panama Route. Some of the travelers entrusted their personal gold to the purser, and others carried gold in closely held personal luggage or in money belts and pouches.

On Thursday, September 3, the *Sonora* reached Panama City. Addie Easton would later recall that "the voyage to the isthmus was one long delight, with smooth waters, sunny skies, and a joyous congenial company." Soon thereafter the passengers were transferred to the Panama Railroad for the four-hour journey by land.

Awaiting the travelers, cargo, and mail at the Aspinwall dock was the ship that would carry them the rest of the way: the United States Mail Steamship *Central America*. Built for the Panama Route during 1852–1853 at the New York shipyard of William H. Webb, the 280-foot-long sidewheel steamer was owned and operated by the United States Mail Steamship Company. Originally christened the *George Law* after one of the firm's owners, the recently renamed ship had completed 43 round-trip voyages between New York and Aspinwall during its four years of operation.

Forty-three-year-old William Lewis Herndon of the United States Navy commanded the vessel in compliance with the law requiring all steamers carrying the U.S. Mail to be captained by a Navy officer. Commander Herndon had achieved national fame in 1851 for leading the first scientific expedition to explore the Amazon River from its source to its mouth. Passengers no doubt looked forward to hearing about his adventures firsthand.

Before the completion of the Panama Railroad in 1855, Panama Route passengers had to make their own precarious way across the isthmus as best they could—on foot, by mule, and in small boats poled down swift rivers by Panamanian guides. The dangerous jungle trek that had taken five miserable days was now a fairly pleasant four-hour tropical excursion.

# William Lewis Herndon: American Hero

"Captain Herndon behaved nobly throughout, and was standing near me on the hurricane deck when she went down. He sank, however, to rise no more, leaving a name to be honored among the heroes of the sea."

— Central America *survivor Oliver Perry Manlove*
Baltimore American *September 21, 1857*

"The Captain's kindness to me, and to all the ladies, was unremitting, and in the end he sacrificed his life for us."

— Central America *survivor Jane Harris*
New York Tribune, *September 21, 1857*

"I believe there was not a man left on board the ship but would have given his life if it could have saved the Captain."

— Central America *survivor Thomas McNeish*
The New-York Times, *September 21, 1857*

**B**orn in Fredericksburg, Virginia, on October 25, 1813, William Lewis Herndon entered the Navy in 1828 and was commissioned lieutenant in 1841. From 1842 to 1847 he served at the United States Naval Observatory and Hydrographic Office in Washington, D.C. There he worked closely with his cousin, brother-in-law, and good friend, Lieutenant Matthew Fontaine Maury, who later became known as "the father of modern oceanography" for his revolutionary studies of winds and water currents.

In 1851, Herndon was assigned to lead the first scientific expedition to explore the Amazon River Valley and three years later published the results in a popular illustrated book, *Exploration of the Valley of the Amazon*. (Among the volume's admirers was a young man named Samuel L. Clemens, who years later, as Mark Twain, claimed reading it had been a turning point in his life. Some scholars have suggested that Twain's *Life on the Mississippi* was inspired in part by Herndon's vivid descriptions.)

In November 1855, Captain Herndon was given command of the *Central America* (then named the *George Law*) in accordance with an act of Congress requiring that all mail steamships be captained by an officer in the U.S. Navy. He completed 18 voyages before the ill-fated trip that began in Aspinwall on September 3, 1857. Herndon was survived by his wife, Frances Hansbrough Herndon, and one daughter, Ellen Lewis Herndon, who later married Chester A. Arthur. (She died, however, before Arthur became the 21st president of the United States.)

The town of Herndon, Virginia, is named in his memory, and in 1858 his native state presented a medal to his widow. In 1860, the United States Naval Academy erected a monument to the captain's memory, making Herndon the first peacetime hero to be so honored at Annapolis.

33D CONGRESS, }     HO. OF REPS.     { EXECUTIVE,
1st Session. }                     { No. 53.

# EXPLORATION

OF THE

# VALLEY OF THE AMAZON,

MADE UNDER DIRECTION OF

# THE NAVY DEPARTMENT,

BY

## WM. LEWIS HERNDON AND LARDNER GIBBON,
LIEUTENANTS UNITED STATES NAVY.

PART I.
BY LIEUT. HERNDON.

WASHINGTON:
ROBERT ARMSTRONG, PUBLIC PRINTER
1854.

*Herndon's book about the Amazon was doubtless the subject of lively shipboard discussions at the captain's table.*

*Far right: The Herndon Monument at the United States Naval Academy in Annapolis, Maryland, was erected in 1860.*

*Near right: In 1858, the State of Virginia posthumously awarded Commander Herndon a medal for his "devotion to duty, Christian conduct, and genuine heroism." The medal was presented to his widow, Frances Hansbrough Herndon.*

At 4:00 PM on September 3, 1857, the *Central America* left Aspinwall, Panama, carrying 578 people, including 477 passengers and 101 crew members. Four days later, the steamer made an intermediate stop in Cuba. "We left Havana at nine o'clock on the morning of the 8th . . . with clear weather and every prospect for a pleasant passage," said J. A. Foster in a later newspaper account. But that prospect began to change on Wednesday, September 9. Virginia Birch was chatting on deck with a group of other female passengers when, as she later remembered, "a squall came up, and the wind blew like a hurricane, and we had to go downstairs."

By Thursday, September 10, merchant captain Thomas W. Badger concurred. "It blew a perfect hurricane and the sea ran mountains high." Although Badger and his wife were passengers on this voyage, he commanded his own bark, the *Jane A. Falkinberg*, back on the West Coast, and he knew a real storm when he saw one.

By that evening, the seas were so rough that most people were sick in their cabins. Judge Alonzo Castle Monson later recalled that "the evening games of cards and other pastimes for diversion and amusement usual in the cabin were dispensed with." This must have been a disappointment to the judge, an inveterate gambler who had once lost his house and all his money in a legendary Sacramento poker game. Earlier during the voyage, Commander Herndon had been Monson's partner at whist; but on this night the commander had more important matters on his mind.

If they slept at all, passengers and crew awoke on Friday to find the storm as violent as before, and possibly even worse. The pounding seas finally began to exact a toll on the laboring vessel's hull. At nine o'clock in the morning, Chief Engineer George Ashby reported that the ship was taking on considerable water. A deadly series of misfortunes plagued the vessel during the hours that followed. The combined effects of the gale and flooding caused it to list to starboard, making it impossible for coal tenders to navigate their wheelbarrows

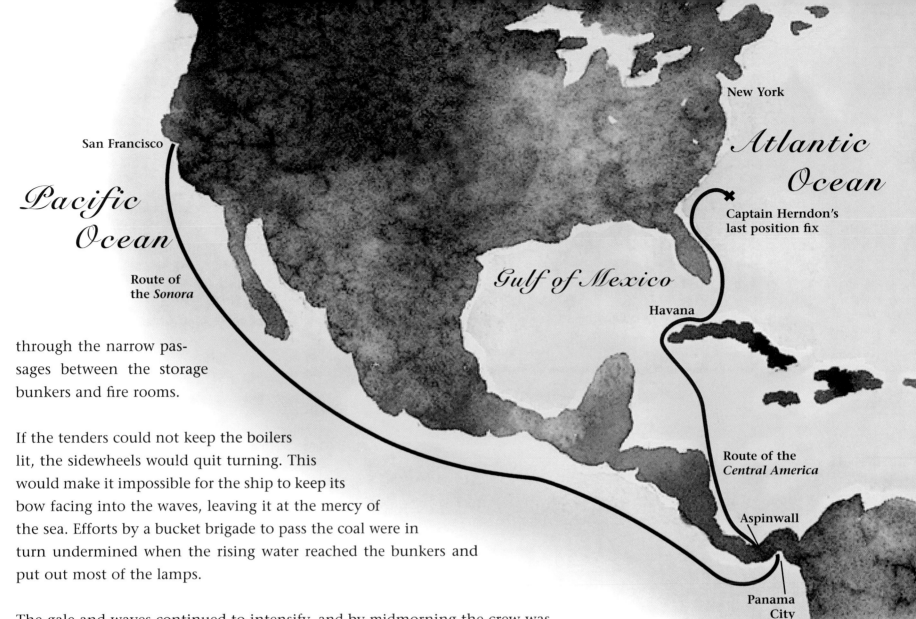

San Francisco

*Pacific Ocean*

Route of the *Sonora*

New York

*Atlantic Ocean*

✖ Captain Herndon's last position fix

*Gulf of Mexico*

Havana

Route of the *Central America*

Aspinwall

Panama City

through the narrow pas-
sages between the storage
bunkers and fire rooms.

If the tenders could not keep the boilers
lit, the sidewheels would quit turning. This
would make it impossible for the ship to keep its
bow facing into the waves, leaving it at the mercy of
the sea. Efforts by a bucket brigade to pass the coal were in
turn undermined when the rising water reached the bunkers and
put out most of the lamps.

The gale and waves continued to intensify, and by midmorning the crew was
no longer able to hold the storm-buffeted steamer on course. At about 10 o'clock
in the morning, the third officer set the storm spencer (the strongest and heav-
iest of all the sails on board), but it soon blew to pieces. By then, reported the
second officer, James Frazer, the ship "was so high out of the water that she
would not head to the wind and sea."

With water rising in the hold, the fire rooms began to flood by late morning.
Further fueling of the fires became impossible. At noon the fire under the starboard boiler went out, and, with steam pressure lost, the starboard engine and
paddlewheel stopped turning. Despite herculean efforts by the coal tenders, at
about three o'clock the fire and engines on the port side also failed. With no
power left, the *Central America* began to wallow helplessly in the sea. The ship
was listing badly. If any passengers still harbored illusions about their safety,

# A Capital Sea Boat

**M**ost of the steamships that served the Panama Route were built in New York City. Along the East River stretched the shipyards of the major builders: Jacob A. Westervelt, William H. Brown, Jeremiah Simonson, and William H. Webb.

From 1840 to 1869, William Webb's shipyard produced 135 vessels, including small fishing craft, oceangoing clippers, and larger steam-powered liners,

including 17 sidewheelers for the Panama Route—more than any other builder. As the head of the enterprise, Webb was both the naval architect and the shipwright, and was known for innovative designs and keen attention to detail. The shipyard later became the Webb Institute, renowned for naval architecture.

On March 25, 1852, the keel was laid for the *George Law*, ordered by the United States Mail Steamship Company. Renamed the *Central America* in 1857, it was a wood-hulled, three-masted sidewheel steamship, about 278 feet long.

*Above: The* New-York Herald *called William H. Webb "the very first true naval architect" in America.*

*Left: This model of the* Central America *was built and presented to Columbus-America by John and Jodi Patton.*

The hull was sheathed with copper plates to protect it from shipworm infestation. Two huge inclined steam engines, built by Morgan Ironworks of New York, drove a pair of midship paddles measuring about 30 feet in diameter. The engine machinery and the massive boilers added 750 tons of ironworks to the total weight of the steamer.

Webb's design also called for an elegant exterior finish. Red paint highlighted the massive sidewheels, housed in black-and-gold paddle boxes. Shiny varnish set off the deck houses to contrast with the black

hull (red below the wale). Masts and bowsprit were natural wood, with spars and cross-trees painted black. A well-planned layout comprised three principal decks. At the top level was the open-air spar (or weather) deck, with the main (or second) deck and the third deck underneath. In the hold below, Webb added smaller, temporary "orlop decks" for cargo. Between the sidewheels was a smaller hurricane deck. First- and second-cabin passengers occupied aft staterooms in the second and third decks. Steerage passengers were forward on the same levels in double tiers of berths. The crew slept in the bow on the second deck, and officers' cabins were on the spar deck.

On October 20, 1853, the *George Law* left on its maiden voyage and thereafter sailed from New York on the 5th or 20th of each month, alternating with other U.S. Mail Steamship Company steamers. Cargo often included important mail and passengers. On its ninth voyage, from Aspinwall to New York in July 1854, for example, the ship carried dispatches from Commodore Matthew Calbraith Perry's expedition to Japan, including the first United States treaty with that country. On its 16th voyage, from New York to Aspinwall in February 1855, guests invited to celebrate the opening of the Panama Railroad were aboard.

After the *Central America* sank, Webb commented on its condition: "She had proved herself during three years' constant service, to be a ship requiring few repairs....I can say that she was pronounced by every one of her commanders and those employed on board of her, to be a capital sea boat, and regarded by nautical men and those capable of judging, as one of the best steamships out of this port."

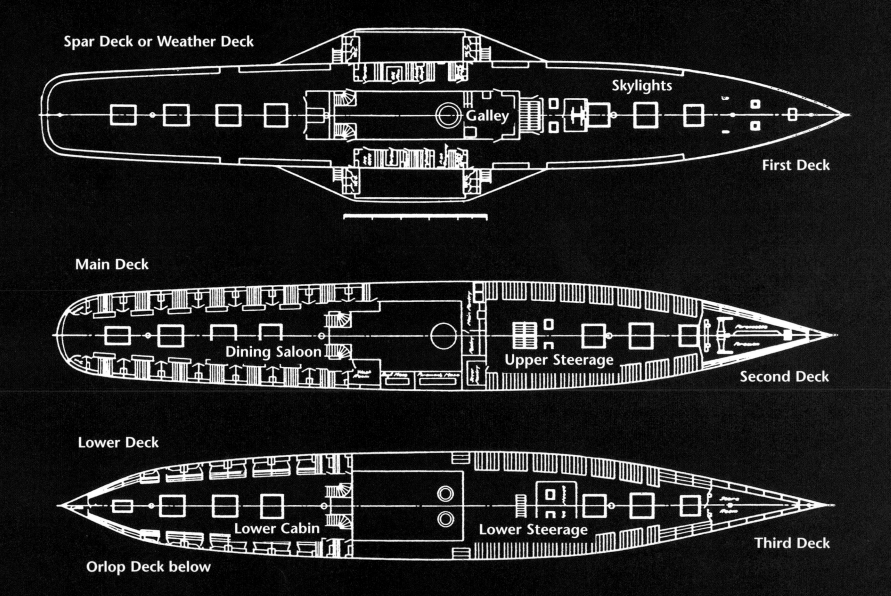

Spar Deck or Weather Deck

Skylights

Galley

First Deck

Main Deck

Dining Saloon

Upper Steerage

Second Deck

Lower Deck

Lower Cabin

Lower Steerage

Third Deck

Orlop Deck below

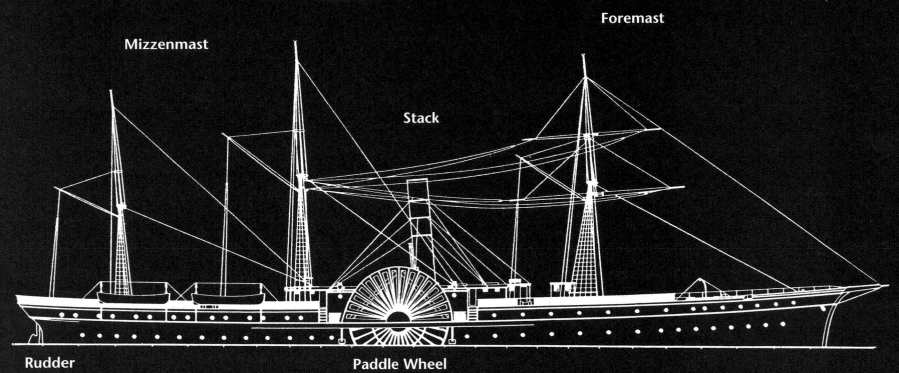

Mizzenmast

Mainmast

Foremast

Stack

Rudder

Paddle Wheel

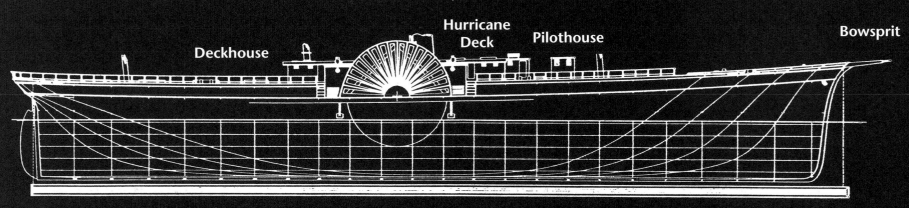

Deckhouse

Hurricane
Deck

Pilothouse

Bowsprit

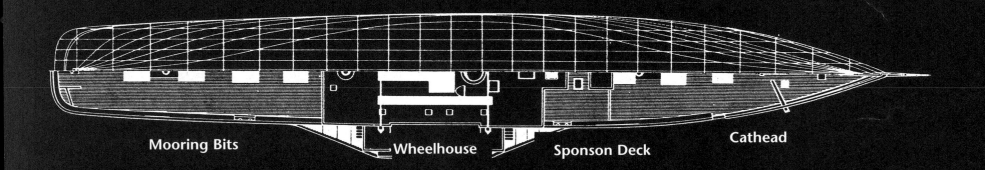

Mooring Bits

Wheelhouse

Sponson Deck

Cathead

these were violently dispelled when, as Addie Easton noted, "the vessel suddenly careened to one side and, looking toward our porthole, I noticed that it was entirely under water."

When the boilers lost steam pressure, the pumps necessary to combat the flooding were in turn rendered useless. Commander Herndon now ordered all the men on board—passengers and crew alike—to assist in bailing the ship. While the men worked, most of the women huddled on the port side of the main cabin, bracing themselves by holding on to furniture.

*A satellite photograph shows Hurricane Hugo in 1989. That storm had essentially the same size and track as the hurricane that sank the* Central America.

"None of us went on the other side of the steamer," said Almira Kittredge, "except once in a while a daring one, like Mrs. Marvin." A young and energetic Chicago woman, Amanda Marvin asked to be allowed to help in the bailing, but, as another passenger, Joseph Bassford, later explained, "the men had too much gallantry to allow this." Virginia Birch and Addie Easton also offered to help and were refused. For 30 hours the men continued their losing battle. Ansel Easton occasionally broke away to sit with Addie. "With clasped hands," she later recalled, "we talked to each other of our dear, dear friends, of our brief happiness together, and our hopes for the future."

At about 11:00 at night, Addie remembered the wedding gifts of crackers and wine that she and Ansel had brought aboard. She distributed them to the men at their posts, prompting grateful passengers to later describe her as "a true angel of mercy."

September 12 brought mixed feelings of relief and dread. Judge Monson recalled that shortly after daybreak, the clouds cleared away somewhat, and the passengers and crew were greatly encouraged. The ship's captain, however, knew better. "Captain Herndon told me then," said Monson, "that there was no hope for us unless the storm abated soon or some vessel hove in sight." Herndon strove to avoid panic, but the severity of the situation was now growing obvious.

"In the course of the day on Saturday it was known by all that the ship was in a sinking condition," recalled Barney Lee. But then, at about noon, a glimmer of hope appeared on the horizon as a brig drew toward the sinking steamship. It was the *Marine*, of Boston, commanded by Captain Hiram Burt, who brought his vessel close under their stern. The *Marine*, however, was lighter than the

*On Friday afternoon, September 11, 1857, Captain Herndon ordered all the men on board, passengers included, to help bail the stricken ship. The bailing continued all day Friday, throughout the night, and right up until the end.*

*Addie Easton shared bottles of wedding-gift wine with the exhausted passengers and crew as they worked to save the ship. Perhaps this was one of her bottles.*

*At about noon on Saturday, September 12, the desperate* Central America *passengers and crew sighted the brig* Marine, *of Boston, captained by Hiram Burt, who promised to do everything he could to help.*

*Central America*, and immediately began to drift downwind, farther and farther away from the distressed vessel. Despite the increasing distance between the two ships, Commander Herndon was determined to save all women and children and ordered the lifeboats launched. The heaving seas immediately swamped two of them, rendering them useless. With great difficulty, the women and older children were lowered by ropes from the *Central America*'s deck into the remaining three lifeboats.

These rose and fell violently with the waves, making the rescue a wet and dangerous affair. Small children were held by their arms above the waves and taken in by the sailors below. Several women dipped into the sea before landing safely. Both Addie Easton and Virginia Birch later lamented that they would never have boarded a lifeboat had they realized that their husbands would not be following close behind them. Other women shared this sentiment, including Annie McNeill, who said, "I should never have left the steamer had I known that the men were not coming. I should never have left my husband."

The last time steerage passenger Mary Swan saw her husband was when he helped her into the boat. "He wanted me to go," she despaired, "and said that he did not care about himself, if it were possible that I could be saved, and the little child." Ada Hawley had an equally tragic memory of her husband, whom she could see as her lifeboat pulled away from the ship: "He stood on the wheel house and kissed his hand to me."

However reluctant they may have been to be separated from their husbands, all the women were transferred to the lifeboats. And all the 29 children aboard were saved except one, a Peruvian boy named Adolphe Oliagne, who may have refused to leave his 21-year-old brother, also on board.

The trip from the *Central America* to the *Marine* through mountainous waves was slow and difficult. Moreover, the two ships had drifted two or three miles apart. "It was fully two hours and a half before we got to the *Marine*," remembered Angeline Bowley. "The water dashed into the boat, and we had to keep dipping it out all the time. Two high waves passed entirely over us, so that it seemed as if we were swamped and sunk; but the boat recovered."

Transferring from lifeboats to the *Marine* was perilous in the raging seas. The *Central America*'s stewardess, pinned between a lifeboat and the brig's hull when the two crashed together, was severely injured and died the following day. Once safely on board the rescue ship, the

*"To get in the lifeboats was a difficult matter, as the waves were so high. However, a noose was made in a rope, and a lady seated herself in it. . . . This process was repeated with all, but many got a ducking, for just as they would be ready to get in a large wave would come, sway the boat from the vessel's side, and of course the lady would go into the water."*
— *Virginia Birch,* Central America *passenger*

Over the next few hours, 100 people were transferred to the Marine in the Central America's lifeboats. On route from Cárdenas, Cuba, to New York, the brig Marine was carrying a cargo of molasses. The ship was owned by Elisha Atkins, of Boston, who was commended by the newspapers of his city for refusing to accept any compensation for services rendered.

rescued women gazed anxiously back toward the steamship *Central America*. "About four o'clock the fog cleared away," remembered Ada Hawley, "and we saw the steamer very distinctly against the sunset clouds; she looked beautiful, and did not seem at all like a sinking ship."

Back on board the steamer, men awaited the lifeboats that returned for them after the women and children were safe. Captain Herndon's orders that all ladies and children should board lifeboats were obeyed to the letter. "The utmost coolness and self-control" had prevailed when the women and children were being transferred, recalled Frank Jones. Not a man attempted to get into the boats. But after the women and children reached safety, he added, it was every man for himself. "When the boats returned . . . the men would throw themselves overboard like sheep, filling them in an instant."

Chief Engineer Ashby took charge of the last lifeboat to leave the sinking steamer, claiming that he had been ordered by Captain Herndon to convince Captain Burt to move closer to the *Central America*. However, upon his arrival at the *Marine*, Ashby learned that the storm had carried away the ship's main yard, main topsail, and jib boom, which prevented it from working its way back toward the steamer. Nobody would row back with Ashby to the sinking steamer, so his life was spared, but some of the passengers branded him a deserter and would have nothing to do with him on the *Marine*.

At about 6:30 PM there was reason for new hope. Another vessel, the schooner *El Dorado* of New York, appeared and sailed to within hailing distance of the *Central America*. But because it had only one very small lifeboat, the schooner was unable to take off any passengers and gradually drifted out of sight of the sinking steamer.

In all, the *Marine* had saved 100 people, but 478 passengers and crewmen still remained on board the *Central America*. Among them were Billy Birch, Ansel

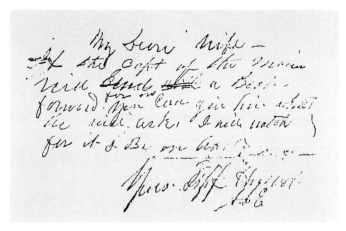

*This note was received on the* Marine *by Adeline Easton from her husband, Ansel, who remained on the* Central America.

*My Dear Wife,*
*If the Capt. of the* Marine *will send a boat forward for me you can give him what he will ask. I will watch for it and be on hand.*
*Your aff [ectionate] Husband,*
*A. I. E.*

*"I had no idea but what my dear husband would be with me in a very short time after I left him. Judge if you can my feelings and intense suffering, as the boats arrived one after another without him. He wrote me a note and sent it by one of the ladies, telling me to offer the Captain of the* Marine *any inducement to send his own boat to the stern of the steamer where he was waiting and watching for it. I, of course, used every entreaty but he said his boat would not live a moment in such a sea."*
— *Adeline Mills Easton*
Central America *passenger*

*Some of those rescued from the* Central America *gather in the cabin of the brig* Marine.

*"The cabin [on board the* Marine*] was about eight feet square. The berths were mostly occupied by children. The rest of us sat around on the floor on anything we could find, or upon nothing. I sat down right by the cabin door, through which the water was rushing in all night. The storm was very high, the sea broke over us, and the ship was tossed to and fro like a feather in a gale. I shall never forget that night. . . ."*

— *Almira Kittredge*
Central America *passenger*

Easton, Oliver Manlove, Rufus Lockwood—and, of course, Commander Herndon, who, following maritime tradition, was determined to be the last to leave his ship or to go down with it. After it became apparent that the ship must surrender to the elements, "the scene among the passengers was one of the most indescribable confusion and alarm," later recalled William Chase, one of those marooned. Many panicked. "The prayers of the pious, the curses of the maddened, and the groans and shrieks of the affrighted," he continued, "were all commingled together, added to which were numerous angry contests between man and man, in many instances amounting to outright fight, for the possession of articles on which to keep themselves afloat in the water."

In the anxiety and terror of the moment, Chase related that "the love of gold was forgotten." Some of the men unbuckled their gold-stuffed belts and flung their hard-earned treasure upon the deck to lighten their weight. Chase claimed that he could easily have picked up thousands of dollars, if he thought he had a chance of reaching safety with this treasure. Shortly before eight o'clock, the *Central America*, with its decks now awash, was rapidly filling with water and sinking lower into the sea. In a dinner conversation earlier in the

voyage Captain Herndon had told the Eastons that if his ship were ever to go down, he would go with it. Now, having done everything he could to save the women and children, and wondering if he could have done anything different to avoid the imminent tragedy, Captain Herndon retired to his quarters. Stoic and proud, he returned to the wheelhouse wearing his full-dress uniform.

According to his friend and fellow captain Thomas Badger, "Captain Herndon took position on the wheel-house with his second officer and fired rockets downward, the usual signal . . . that we were sinking rapidly. This was a fearful moment, and must have been also to the ladies on board the *Marine*."

Survivors recalled that the vessel lurched three times, with passengers jumping off at each lurch. Those who jumped off at the first and second lurches swam off, but most remained on deck until the vessel went down a minute or two later. "A rocket shot out obliquely," remembered Addie Easton, who was

*Female passengers saved from the* Central America *rest on the deck of the brig* Marine.

*"My brig being disabled, heavily laden and very wet, and, owing to the want of accommodations on board my vessel, the cabin being small and cramped could not accommodate more than six or eight persons, consequently the remaining number were obliged to lie on deck, exposed to the sea and spray, which was constantly breaking over her. . . . The ladies particularly displayed the greatest firmness and heroism, making no complaint, and content to suffer any and all deprivations."*
*— Captain Hiram Burt of the brig* Marine

watching from the *Marine*. "The lights disappeared beneath the waves, and all the world grew dark for me." She had no way of knowing it, but Ansel was standing next to Captain Herndon when the rockets shot into the sky.

The ship plunged at a 45-degree angle, related another account, and then disappeared. As it slipped down, the enormous suction generated by the sinking vessel pulled the men on board far below the surface. Those who managed to fight their way back above water were greeted by a horrifying scene: "Men, some holding planks, and others without anything, were tossed about through the sea for a great space, and appeared to me like so many corks," recalled Barney Lee. "The cries of despair which were uttered by all faintly reached me. I could not describe my feelings at this awful moment."

Through the night the survivors were battered about in the darkness, sometimes in groups, sometimes alone. Bodies floated in the water. "I struck against many of them," related one survivor, John C. Taylor. "They were all provided with life-preservers, yet dead, and with their heads down in the water. It was a horrible sight."

Some of those still alive tried to help others. According to a newspaper account, Billy Birch, the minstrel star, courageously went into his act to buoy up sinking hopes, mimicking sea monsters and telling humorous stories. "Nor did he cease his vivifying harangue," said the paper, "until an overwhelming billow [temporarily] choked his utterance." Shortly after midnight on the morning of September 13, the storm finally began to abate and the sea calmed. The Norwegian bark *Ellen* neared the area where the *Central America* had gone down. Unaware of the tragedy, its captain, Anders Johnsen, had just changed course when a small bird flew across the ship once or twice, and then darted into his face.

He took no notice at first, but when the bird went through the same maneuver twice more, the captain decided it must be an omen. "Upon this I was induced

*When it became apparent that the* Central America *could not be saved, Commander Herndon stood on the wheelhouse, firing rockets to signal the imminent sinking. That must have been a dreadful moment for those watching from the* Marine, *many of whom had husbands, fathers, and friends still aboard the steamer.*

At 8:00 PM on Saturday, September 12, 1857, the Central America sank, going down at an angle of 45 degrees, stern first. The enormous suction pulled the men underwater for some distance. Those lucky enough to resurface were tossed like corks in the roiling water, as shown in a lithograph published by J. Childs of Philadelphia.

"At the time of the going down of the steamer there arose a hoarse yell, as if coming from the bottom of the ocean, and in a moment all was over."
— *Enrique Ayulo*
*Central America*
*passenger*

65

This engraving from Frank Leslie's Illustrated Newspaper *was taken from a sketch by one of the surviving passengers.*

*"On rising to the surface the scenes presented were horrifying—men, some holding planks, and others without anything, were tossed about through the sea for a great space, and appeared to me like so many corks, while the cries of despair which were uttered by all faintly reached me. I could not describe my feelings at this awful moment."*
— Barney M. Lee Central America passenger

*A raft, part of the* Central America's *hurricane deck, carries the living, the dead, and the dying away from the site of the sinking. Among the men were Alexander Grant and George Dawson.*

to re-alter my course into the original one, which I had been steering, and in a short time I heard voices, and on trying to discover where they proceeded from, discovered that I was in the midst of people who had been shipwrecked."

At about one o'clock in the morning, five hours after the *Central America* sank, Captain Johnsen's crew began pulling men from the ocean. By nine o'clock they had saved 50. The crew of the *Ellen* continued to search for survivors until noon that day, then set sail for Norfolk, Virginia. Coincidentally, the *Marine* was also en route to Norfolk with its survivors.

Nine days later, three more men—passenger George Dawson, crew member Alexander Grant, and first assistant engineer John Tice—were found barely alive in one of the *Central America*'s lifeboats, which had drifted away from the *Marine* and been discovered by the three desperate men. Ultimately, 153 were rescued and an estimated 425 died. Billy Birch and Ansel Easton were among the fortunate men rescued by the *Ellen* and were soon reunited with their brides. Merchant captain Thomas Badger also rejoined his wife after being saved by the same ship. But 12 other unfortunate couples were denied a happy reunion. "I have no friend in New York, nor in all the world," passenger Mary Swan grieved, "now that my husband is lost."

Oliver Perry Manlove, the young poet, was among those who made it aboard the *Ellen,* although the poems he had written in California were lost. Undaunted by his ordeal, Oliver soon embarked on new adventures. His unpublished memoirs vividly detail his voyage on the ill-fated *Central America*. Rufus A. Lockwood, the eccentric attorney, did not survive. However, his wife was reportedly so used to his absences that for years afterward she fully expected him to reappear.

*Dawson and Grant, the last survivors on the raft, sighted one of the* Central America's *lifeboats on the fifth day of their ordeal. Grant swam to it, and in it discovered John Tice. The two rowed back and rescued Dawson.*

# Birch, Dawson, and the Silver Cup

*Above: James E. Birch was a pioneer stagecoach entrepreneur and president of the San Antonio and San Diego Mail Line. Ironically, the first mail reached San Diego on September 8, 1857, just four days before Birch died on the* Central America.

*Right: An advertisement details the routes of Birch's stage service.*

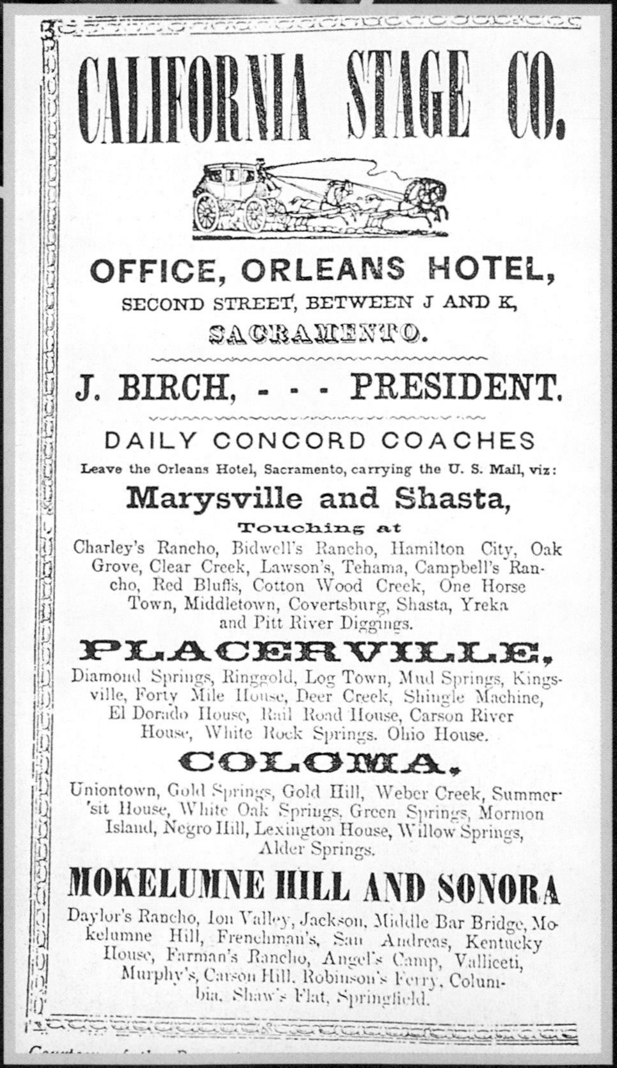

**CALIFORNIA STAGE CO.**

OFFICE, ORLEANS HOTEL,

SECOND STREET, BETWEEN J AND K,

**SACRAMENTO.**

**J. BIRCH, - - - PRESIDENT.**

DAILY CONCORD COACHES

Leave the Orleans Hotel, Sacramento, carrying the U. S. Mail, viz:

**Marysville and Shasta,**

Touching at

Charley's Rancho, Bidwell's Rancho, Hamilton City, Oak Grove, Clear Creek, Lawson's, Tehama, Campbell's Rancho, Red Bluffs, Cotton Wood Creek, One Horse Town, Middletown, Covertsburg, Shasta, Yreka and Pitt River Diggings.

**PLACERVILLE,**

Diamond Springs, Ringgold, Log Town, Mud Springs, Kingsville, Forty Mile House, Deer Creek, Shingle Machine, El Dorado House, Rail Road House, Carson River House, White Rock Springs. Ohio House.

**COLOMA,**

Uniontown, Gold Springs, Gold Hill, Weber Creek, Summer 'sit House, White Oak Springs, Green Springs, Mormon Island, Negro Hill, Lexington House, Willow Springs, Alder Springs.

**MOKELUMNE HILL AND SONORA**

Daylor's Rancho, Ion Valley, Jackson, Middle Bar Bridge, Mokelumne Hill, Frenchman's, San Andreas, Kentucky House, Farman's Rancho, Angel's Camp, Valliceti, Murphy's, Carson Hill. Robinson's Ferry, Columbia, Shaw's Flat, Springfield.

Twenty-nine-year-old James Birch traveled overland to California with the first wave of the gold rush in 1849. But, unlike many Forty-Niners, Birch never intended to strain his back over a prospector's pan. Having driven stage" in his native New England, he headed for Sacramento with plans to establish a stage service (fares due in cash or gold dust) to carry miners to and from the gold camps.

By 1854, the handsome young Birch had been named president of the new state's largest stage operation. "Birch's horses . . . dashed through sloughs and gulches in a remarkably knowing style," reported a *Sacramento Placer Times* reporter of his ride on one of the stages. "Birch's Line [is] the line to get to the mines in a hurry."

Despite this success, it wasn't long before the entrepreneur saw greater opportunity in transporting mail than prospectors. At the time, the only regularly scheduled mail between the coasts went by steamship, although the U.S. Post Office routed some mail overland by way of Fort Leavenworth, Kansas, and Santa Fe, New Mexico.

In July 1857, Birch formed the San Antonio and San Diego Mail Line, securing the contract for the western leg of the nation's first regularly scheduled cross-country mail.

Although it would be known by some as the "Jackass Mail" for the pack mules that carried mail sacks over one 180-mile stretch, he was elated with his success. But Birch missed the family he had left behind in Swansea, Massachusetts. Carrying a silver cup as a present for a young son, he boarded the *Central America* September 3, 1857, bound for New York, yet he would never live to deliver the cup personally.

As the steamer was about to sink, Birch became despondent over his chances for survival. He called on an acquaintance and fellow passenger, George Dawson, and entrusted his silver cup to him. Dawson, a free African American, had been working as a porter at the

70

St. Nicholas Hotel in Oroville, California. The hotel was a depot for Birch's stage company, and the two had probably met there.

George Dawson was one of two men left alive on a raft. He later joined another man who was alone in one of the steamer's lifeboats. Eight days and 20 hours after the sinking, the three were rescued by the British brig *Mary*. After returning to New York, Dawson found James Birch's widow, Julia, and presented the silver cup to her, faithfully honoring the pledge he had made to her husband.

*George Dawson, a free African American, was rescued after nine harrowing days at sea. Honoring his promise to James Birch, he managed to keep Birch's silver cup safe throughout his long ordeal.*

*Columbus-America researchers used survivor accounts published in 1857 newspapers such as* Frank Leslie's Illustrated Newspaper *to find clues about the location of the* Central America *shipwreck.*

Most prominent among those who died was the *Central America*'s captain, William Lewis Herndon. The country hailed him for his orderly rescue of the women and children and his courage in remaining with his ship to the last. He received a moving tribute from his brother-in-law, Lieutenant Matthew Fontaine Maury, the father of the science of oceanography and the Navy's top expert in the field. "Forgetful of self, mindful of others, his life was beautiful to the last," wrote Maury, "and in his death he added a new glory to the annals of the sea."

Accounts of the disaster hummed over telegraph wires up and down the eastern seaboard. The press dwelled on the tragedy for months, calling for investigations and speculating about the causes. Editorials demanded greater safety at sea and pressed for construction of a transcontinental railroad to ensure safe land passage.

The news also fanned the sparks of a financial decline. Banks, which backed their notes with gold, were increasingly worried about a run as depositors began to exchange their notes for gold and reserves dropped to their lowest point of the year in late August. The loss of the commercial gold shipments aboard the *Central America* was a blow to banks in the East, and by mid-October banking firms were closing throughout the region and many other businesses across the country were failing.

The tragedy of the *Central America* was soon eclipsed by the Civil War, and passed into legend. But the final chapter of the story was not yet written.

# News of the Event

News of the *Central America* disaster first reached land on September 17, 1857, when Captain Post of the *Thomas Swann* landed in Charleston, South Carolina. While still at sea, Captain Post had spoken with Captain Johnsen of the bark *Ellen,* en route to Norfolk, Virginia, with 50 *Central America* survivors.

Thanks to the telegraph system, this first word of the disaster was immediately relayed to cities all along the eastern seaboard. Newspaper articles appeared in New York, Boston, Baltimore, and Philadelphia on the morning of Friday, September 18—before a single survivor had been interviewed. By the next day, people in cities as far west as Madison, Wisconsin, were reading about the *Central America* disaster in their own hometown papers.

On the morning of September 18, survivors landed in Norfolk, Virginia, and in Savannah, Georgia, and immediately found themselves the center of attention. Reporters were eager for all the details the eyewitnesses could provide and took advantage of the telegraph to tell the story of the *Central America* tragedy, relaying a steady stream of survivor accounts and editorial speculation to the news-hungry population.

The first transcontinental telegraph was not completed until 1861, however, which was four years after the *Central America* disaster. Californians—many of whom had friends and relatives on board the ship—did not learn about the sinking until October 22, when the tragic news finally arrived by steamship.

UNION.

...OO NEWS.

...oat.

—*Melancholy* ...tement of the ...*robable Num-*

2—3¼ P. M.

h arrived this ...e most heart- ...since the dis- ...irely absorbs ...ity; nothing ...ly announced ...a dispatch to ...on board the ...t Havana un- ...oss of life by

...R, SECOND

...Havana, Sept. ..., steering for ...erate breezes

...nd head sea; ..., distance 15 ...sh breeze and ...on, but don't

**BY TELEGRAPH TO THE UNION.**

BY THE STATE TELEGRAPH LINE.

[From the Extra Union of Thursday.]

## ARRIVAL OF THE
## STEAMER PANAMA.

TWO WEEKS LATER FROM THE ATLANTIC.

### AWFUL DISASTER AT SEA!

**Total Loss of the California Mail Steamer CENTRAL AMERICA, With her Mails, Treasure, and a large portion of her Passengers.**

## FOUR HUNDRED AND FORTY LIVES LOST!

One hundred and seventy-three persons rescued!

THE WOMEN AND CHILDREN SAVED!

About Two Millions of Treasure Lost!

ARRIVAL OF THE SAVED IN NEW YORK!

Settlement of the New Granada Difficulty—Large California Land Sale—Election in Maine, &c.

SAN FRANCISCO, Oct. 22, 8 A. M.

The Pacific Mail Steamship Company's steamer

19th Septen ...with the o ...them all on ...Sunday, Sep

The follo ...persons kno ...almost comp ...picked up b ...not in the li

Alford He ...Ashby Ge ...Agulo C., ...Adams W ...Athronsah ...Badger Ca ...Bennett L ...Bliss Wm. ...Bassford, ...Brumwell ...Badgeley ...Borew Lev ...Bailey Mrs ...Birch Mrs. ...Bride Thor ...Brown Ed ...Brougham ...Bruyne Ge ...Black John ...Burt Hirar ...Badger Mr ...Brown Mr

*Because the national telegraph system did not yet extend across the Mississippi, Californians did not learn about the September 12 disaster until more than a month later.*

# CHAPTER THREE
# EXPLORERS OF THE DEEP

*In the mid-1980s, Tommy Thompson, an ocean engineer employed in scientific research at the prestigious research and development firm Battelle Memorial Institute, took a leave of absence to develop the systems and technology for finding and recovering shipwrecks in the deep ocean. Three years later he found the legendary United States Mail Steamship* Central America *and subsequently recovered it.*

Ever since my youth, I have been fascinated by the black, frigid, sea depths below 600 feet known as the "deep ocean." This lightless void covers two thirds of the planet, yet we have seen only one ten-thousandth of it. In volume, it constitutes an enormous amount of the planet's biological habitat, yet we have virtually no knowledge of the vast variety of sea creatures that inhabit it. Neither sun nor diver has been able to penetrate depths more than half a mile. Although just under the surface where ships pass every day, the deep ocean has remained as far from humankind as the reaches of outer space.

While in college studying ocean engineering, I realized that shipwrecks, with their mystery, their historical value, and in many cases their treasure, might lure entrepreneurs and explorers off the shore and serve as the stepping stones into the deep ocean. In 1977, I began extensive research into historic deep-ocean shipwrecks—none of which had ever been photographed or imaged on sonar—and studied various methods and technologies used to find ships sunk in shallow water. Having developed a list of vessels lost in deep water that met a basic set of criteria and might be recoverable with the right plan and the right technology, I set out to find the United States Mail Steamship *Central America* in 1981.

The *Central America* had long suggested itself as an intriguing target. The sinking was well documented by survivors' reports that could be analyzed for clues to the ship's location. The sidewheeler was far enough off the coast to be in deep water, which meant that technology, not luck, would play the most important role in finding and recovering it. The *Central America* was deep enough to remain undisturbed by storms, tides, and other natural phenomena that can disperse a shipwreck over many miles of ocean floor. And

*Overleaf: The engine works of the* **Central America** *are still in place on the shipwreck between the two sidewheels. A cylinder, upper right, cylinder rod, center, and cross head-connecting rod assembly, lower center, can be seen.*

Left: Some people survived the storm by grabbing onto pieces of debris from the ship. Gulfstream currents kept the water relatively warm.

Below: This article in the New-York Daily Tribune was published on October 6, 1857, and told the story of the arrival of the final three survivors from the Central America in New York.

there was enough documented treasure on board to induce partners to sponsor an expedition.

As my research into the hundreds of newspaper accounts of the *Central America*'s demise intensified, the quantity of information became almost overwhelming. Detailed interviews with survivors and with passengers and crew members from nearby ships often covered entire front pages of contemporary newspapers. These provided a vast array of perspectives on exactly what happened during the three-day hurricane that had doomed the *Central America* nearly a century and a half earlier.

But a system for organizing and analyzing the information was needed. An understanding of the geology of that

## THE GREAT WRECK.

### Three more Survivors.

Rescue of Messrs. John Tice, Alex. Grant, and J. W. Dawson by the British brig Mary.

### STATEMENTS OF THEIR SUFFERINGS.

### Eight Days and Twenty Hours without Food or Drink.

"Three more saved from the Central America," was the announcement that was made by the ship news reporter at 9 o'clock yesterday morning, as he stepped from the Staten Island ferry-boat at White-hall; and his words were echoed from one to another until nearly all in the lower part of the city were

# Data Correlation Matrix

The Columbus-America data correlation matrix was used to compare and evaluate 33 accounts of the sinking given by survivors and eyewitnesses to the *Central America* disaster. The descriptions, mainly from 1857 newspapers, came from a diverse group of people with widely differing experiences. A judge, several merchants, three women, one teenager, miners, crew members, the captains and passengers of the rescue ships, and a meteorological expert all left important historical clues concerning the steamer's location.

These were entered into the data correlation matrix, created on a 12-by-12-foot sheet of paper.

Within the matrix, the 33 historical accounts are arranged into three-hour time slots covering the period of the storm and shipwreck, allowing easy comparison of the different stories at specific points in time. The time slots are arranged down the left side and the names of the witnesses run across the top.

The matrix contains information relating to the weather, such as the progress of the hurricane, and to the physical circumstances of sinking, including the deteriorating condition of the steamship. This data was used by search theory mathematicians to construct the probability maps that allowed for eventual discovery of the shipwreck.

| | Surviving Officers' Combined Account | Virginia Birch, First Cabin Passenger | Alonzo C. Monson, First Cabin Passenger, Judge of the 6th Federal District, California |
|---|---|---|---|
| **Saturday, 9/12** | | | |
| **12:00 P.M.** | About noon a vessel hove in sight-- the brig *Marine*.<br><br>Brig rounded to under steamer's lee at about 2 o'clock or a little thereafter. Three lifeboats successfully launched. | On Saturday at 12:00, a brig was seen some little distance. It bore down toward us. | At half past one a sail was seen in the distance. |
| **3:00 P.M.** | By the time the boats reached the brig the second time, she had drifted five miles to the leeward.<br><br>At 4:00, main spencer set to try to keep up with the brig in drifting. | | After the women and children were aboard the brig, he boarded lifeboat with Mr. Priest . "As we started for the brig the distance was two miles. By the time we reached her it was 3 miles. It took an hour and a half to reach the brig." In about a half hour, a small boat came, with Ashby and others on board. Shortly, two boats came up, with passengers and firemen aboard. |
| **6:00 P.M.** | Black's boat reaches the steamer about 7:30. Steamer sending up rockets. Hailed by Captain Herndon and told to keep off.<br><br>At about 8 o'clock P.M. or a few minutes thereafter, the ship settled | All who were rescued were on board the brig by 6:00.<br><br>Towards evening we saw a schooner close.<br><br>It soon became dark. | Schooner and steamer's lights visible from the *Marine*. "Shortly after, the steamer's lights disappeared." |

part of the ocean in which the ship likely lay would also increase understanding of the challenges the *Central America* would present to search and recovery.

In 1983, as my interest in exploring the deep ocean was intensifying, I enlisted the help of Bob Evans, a longtime associate, who was a consulting geologist for the state of Ohio. Bob is also a trivia and history buff and has a steel-trap mind that seems to retain every fact he has ever learned. We are both drawn to unusual projects and to what I call "thought experiments." And, perhaps most important, Bob is wonderful company, effusive and enthusiastic where I am more reserved and analytical. Together we spent many evenings in animated discussions about inventions, innovation, and exploration.

Bob and I compiled the extensive passenger and crew information into what we termed a "data correlation matrix." On a 12-by-12-foot sheet of paper we entered every comment, every observation, every fact that might offer some insight as to where the ship might have been when it disappeared beneath the waves at 8:00 PM on Saturday, September 12, 1857.

*Above: Bob Evans, Columbus-America's Director of Science and History, usually serves as mission coordinator in the control room. He is in charge of planning each dive, overseeing its execution, logging recovered objects, and making scientific observations.*

We took the matrix to Dr. Lawrence D. Stone, one of the world's leading experts on search theory, a method using probability and statistical analysis to find objects, particularly in the ocean. He had helped locate the U.S. nuclear submarine *Scorpion* lost in the Atlantic in 1968 and was impressed with the information we had gathered about the *Central America*.

Although no one had previously applied search theory to a historical database like our matrix, Larry proceeded to create thousands of computerized models of possible sinking scenarios based on variables such as the *Central America*'s last known coordinates, the hurricane's probable wind speed and direction, and likely ocean currents at the time of the disaster. Ultimately, he came up with a 1,400-square-mile search area (larger than the state of Rhode Island).

*Long months aboard the research vessel leave time for contemplating the horizon.*

I first shared my plans—and my belief that the *Central America* could be found and recovered—with my former professor at Ohio State, Dr. Donald Glower, who had become dean of Ohio State's College of Engineering. An important mentor, Don had encouraged my ocean-engineering studies. He was not at all daunted by the prospect of attempting something never before done and helped open the door for me to the leaders of the Columbus business community.

As the project developed, I knew we would need assistance in communications from someone who understood and could work with the media. Again, the right person was at hand. I called Barry Schatz, a boyhood friend from Defiance, Ohio, who was working as an editor in Gainesville, Florida. While Bob continued historical research and Barry helped write up the findings and the preliminary business plan, I set out to find sponsors.

The biggest boost came from Wayne Ashby, the managing partner of the Columbus office of a major national accounting firm and one of the most respected financial minds in the community. After listening carefully for many months and asking many questions, Wayne came to believe we could succeed in our endeavor. He helped organize a small core group of partners, enlisted legal advice from the local law firm of Porter, Wright, Morris & Arthur, and helped me structure a partnership known as the Columbus-America Discovery Group. During the next three years, the enterprise would grow to 161 partners investing more than $10 million in different phases and a team of some 40 scientists, engineers, and technicians.

Initial financing was in hand by 1986. We chartered an old Louisiana mud boat, the *Pine River*, for a grueling 40-day sonar search through the target areas gridded by Larry Stone in the Atlantic Ocean. During this stage we used a

# Search Theory/Composite Probability Map

Search theory is a mathematical specialty dealing with objects lost at sea. It is used to create a map of the distribution of probable locations based on the available data and has many modern applications. The Coast Guard uses search theory for search and rescue operations, for example, while other government agencies employ the method to look for downed air- and spacecraft and to track enemy submarines.

Search theory was also used to locate the *Central America*. First, numerical values were assigned to information from the accounts of the shipwreck charted on the data correlation matrix. Currents, winds, and vessel condition all factored into the calculations.

Close analysis of the historical records showed that several different sinking scenarios needed evaluation. One of these was based on Captain Herndon's final navigational fix. Alternate scenarios drew on the observations and opinions of other ships' captains in the vicinity at the time of the storm. Complex formulas made it possible to analyze the data and simulate a range of sinking scenarios. Finally, computer simulations were run thousands of times in order to produce a distribution of probable locations for the shipwreck.

The results of the calculations are shown on this composite probability map, which was critical to the search plan. Higher and lower numbers represent areas of higher and lower probability. Each number designates an area of ocean floor four nautical miles square. The Xs indicate the positions given by Herndon, Badger, and the captains of the *Marine* and the *Ellen*. Long straight paths with arrows show the direction in which the plan moves. Starting near the bottom center of the figure, it searches the high probability areas first, then systematically works its way out to the others.

# Sea MARC Sonar

The Sea MARC sonar used by the Columbus-America Discovery Group to locate the *Central America* is a side-scanning device that is towed behind the surface vessel in swaths while sending out a strong pulse of sound waves to detect objects on the ocean floor. A computer aboard the research vessel interprets the returning signals and "paints" an image of the seabed. After one sweep, the vessel turns 180 degrees and maps a band parallel to the previous one, overlapping the passes to eliminate any possible gaps in the record. This systematic process is known as "mowing the lawn."

When the sonar passes over an anomaly, the image registers in changing tones and colors. A shipwreck stands out prominently in such a side-scan sonar image. The hard hull of the ship returns a strong signal shown in oranges and reds. The greens and blues are background colors. The dark "shadow" indicates a very weak or absent signal, caused when the wreck obscures the sea floor behind it.

newly available technology known as Sea MARC side-scanning sonar, which we had modified, to sweep the grid in three-mile swaths. The Sea MARC produced a set of sonogram pictures used to identify anomalies, or anything that stands out from the sea floor: rock formations, trash from a passing ship, a tree that has drifted hundreds of miles from the shore, downed planes, shipwrecks. Special computer software was devised to bring out features indicating a ship, and, we hoped, the *Central America*.

Because the sonograms appear in "real time," or at the same moment the sonar passes over the anomalies, the temptation to explore each one was strong. Stopping, however, was a luxury we could not afford. The 40-day period covering the equipment lease and employment of sonar operators did not provide much time to cover the entire grid. Horrendous weather slowed us even more. We had to keep moving to finish exploring the area. During the next weather window the following summer we could return to make detailed analyses of the most promising sites.

The weather window, or optimum period of good weather and calm seas, runs roughly from June to early October. Winter is a time for analyzing, planning, and retooling. The winter of 1986–1987 in Columbus was devoted to two things: analyzing the sonar images from the previous summer and developing the technology that had been my vision for years. This was *Nemo*, an undersea robot specially designed for historic shipwreck excavation using archaeological techniques, known in ocean-engineering circles as a remotely operated vehicle (ROV). If *Nemo,* the centerpiece of the expedition, functioned as envisioned, it would be capable of extended, heavy-duty, and complex work in the deep ocean's harsh environment and thus establish mankind's first "working presence" more than a mile and a half down.

I explained my design concepts to several people, including Don Hackman, a former colleague at Battelle Memorial Institute and one of the world's foremost ocean engineers. Together we began to build a robot that was fitted with manipulator arms, cameras, and lights that could explore the ocean while operated by scientists and engineers aboard an attending research vessel.

In 1987, we retrofitted another workboat, the *Nicor Navigator*, and returned to the site our over-the-winter image analysis had indicated as the most promising. All the hard work seemed to pay off early in the season, when the robot's cameras revealed what appeared to be mid-19th-century artifacts, including china, pitchers, washbowls, and toys, amidst a rotting wood hull—the first ever seen in the deep ocean. It was humbling to be staring at these very personal effects, to know that they were the aftermath of some unutterable tragedy.

*Bob Evans looks for pirates, bad weather, and the overdue supply boat.*

But there was little time for wonder. The weather window was closing, our partners were waiting for news of success, and costs were mounting daily. Our imaging technology had proved capable, but we still had to determine whether this was the right site. And if it was, a complex and lengthy recovery lay ahead. We also faced pressure from another front. Even before we arrived at the shipwreck site in 1987, competitors appeared in the area. Although we doubted that they had the technology to make a recovery in deep water, we were concerned that they might image the site and try to interfere with our operations.

To protect the site legally from these other groups, maritime attorney Rick Robol advised us to retrieve an item to prove that Columbus-America had been present on—and was legally in control of—the still-unidentified shipwreck. We wanted to avoid disturbing the site and valuable artifacts, so after long deliberation we decided to bring up a lump of coal. With some difficulty and some luck, *Nemo* was able to retrieve several pieces in its first attempt at deep-ocean recovery.

Time was of the essence. Competitors were surveying with sonar, and it was critically important to get the coal to a courtroom quickly in order to stake a claim. However, to our dismay, heaving seas made it impossible for the Columbus-America seaplane to land in the water. Communicating by satellite, our pilot,

Steve Gross, and I came up with a plan. We wrapped our prize securely in duct tape and hung it on a rope strung between the *Nicor Navigator* and a mast on our dinghy, which I had paddled about 50 yards away. A moment later, Gross swept through in our Seabee seaplane, snatched the package with a grappling hook, and was off to Norfolk, Virginia.

*Although the RV* Arctic Discoverer *does not look like a high-tech research vessel from the outside, inside it has state-of-the-art navigational, communications, and electronics systems.*

There, within about four hours of its recovery from the ocean floor, our attorneys presented the lump of coal in federal district court and won an injunction on the site. This was the first time such a claim had ever been made to a shipwreck touched only by a robot. The ruling set precedent in international maritime law since the injunction was granted on the basis of a new legal concept called "telepresence," in which the remote, or "virtual" presence made possible by *Nemo*'s unique technology was recognized as proper grounds for the claim.

I was excited about our achievements but knew the partnership needed some definitive accomplishments. During the winter of 1987–1988, Columbus-America and a few partners demonstrated continued support by purchasing an old Canadian icebreaker, the *Arctic Discoverer*, which was retrofitted for the final search and recovery. We were happy to be making the final push with a ship of our own, designed to our specifications.

The 1988 weather window opened with another frustrating delay. We had to wait most of the summer for the outboard thrusters, critical in keeping the research vessel positioned over the shipwreck site. We finally arrived in Wilmington, North Carolina. It was August—very late in the season—before we were able to steam out of port with a crew of about 25.

# RV *Arctic Discoverer*

Thirty years old and a thousand miles from her native waters, the Research Vessel *Arctic Discoverer* herself might appear to be from another place and time. When the old icebreaker rides high and proud in the Atlantic currents, just outside of the Gulf Stream, she seems a faded matron of the seas. There is little evidence at first glance that her humble exterior conceals a sophisticated system of computers, communications equipment, satellite links, and robotic controls.

*Above: On any ship at sea there can be only one person in charge of day-to-day operations. On the RV* Arctic Discoverer *it is Captain Bill Burlingham—for whom the phrase "he runs a tight ship" must have been invented.*

At the beginning of the project, the research vessel was one of a very small percentage of the world's vessels that was equipped to hold its place above a deep-ocean site via a global positioning system. This GPS is able to hold a precise position by processing signals from three fixed satellites designed to return the signals to an onboard computer. Special software sends instructions to two massive outboard thrusters mounted on the ship's starboard side. These mechanical devices make slight corrections forward and backward to keep the ship automatically positioned within 18 feet of a point on the ocean floor 8,000 feet below, even in heavy weather.

Deep within her bow, in the tiny control room under the main deck, a dozen whirring computers keep a continuous vigil on the ocean floor. One monitor displays 3-D images that require viewers to don special glasses. Elsewhere on board, labs contain the latest equipment for preserving biological samples and conserving coins. A host of ship-to-shore communications devices keeps the crew in touch with the outside world.

On the main deck, a winch and crane spool 14,000 feet of coaxial fiber-optic cable into the Atlantic. A mile and a half below, *Nemo* silently goes about its business of scientific sampling and gold recovery.

And in a low-tech touch that is characteristic of the project, a vintage 1957 Italian twin-engine seaplane keeps the crew supplied with necessities during the long summer months at sea.

*Above and left: When waves wash the deck of the RV Arctic Discoverer during a storm, crew members cannot help but think of the hurricane that sank the Central America. It is difficult to imagine being on a 19th-century wood-hulled steamship in waters so high and violent.*

Once the RV Arctic Discoverer reaches the shipwreck site, it generally does not return to port for several weeks. Sealed into a watertight container that is dropped from the plane into the sea, mail and small packages are delivered by airplane. Top left: The container, about to be dropped, is visible just below the plane's partially opened door. Above left and left: Crew members go by dinghy to retrieve a watertight mail canister. Above: Larger items, such as equipment parts, are delivered by supply boat.

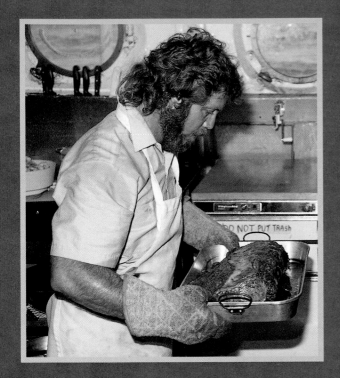

Above, left and right: One of the most important crew members on any ship at sea is the chef. On the Arctic Discoverer, that role is admirably filled by Mickey King. As the chef explains it, "It takes hours to prepare this food, but it only takes the crew five minutes to eat it."

Left: The crew takes time out to pose for a photograph.

*Above and opposite: Driven by auxiliary engines installed on the aft deck, bow and stern thrusters are used to maintain position—within 18 feet—directly over the shipwreck site. Each thruster is omni-directional and linked by a computer to a satellite navigation system.*

Without definitive proof that we had found the *Central America* the previous summer, Bob Evans had spent a good part of the winter reanalyzing some of the other targets the 1986 sonar survey had turned up. This time, we were armed with new image-processing software and another season's experience in image reading and had become increasingly intrigued by an anomaly at another site. The ocean floor is surprisingly littered with both geological and man-made clutter, and the new anomaly could have been anything—a ditched plane, for example, or an unusual rock formation. Since it was closer to shore than the previous summer's site, we decided to stop on the way out and take a closer look, if only to test *Nemo* and the equipment on the *Arctic Discoverer* and to do comparison studies with the other site.

On Sunday, September 11, we were all weary as we finally lowered *Nemo* over the side and into the water to begin its descent to the bottom. Everyone felt the effects of months of shore mobilization and days of dive preparation and equipment tuning. Every dive is preceded by this work. But given that this was the first of the season and some of us still lacked sea legs from the long journey out, it was even more difficult than usual.

A few hours after the underwater robot reached the bottom, five of us sat in the control room deep inside the hull of the *Arctic Discoverer* staring at the images of the soundless seascape projected through the blue half-light of 12 video monitors. This can become almost meditative, but eventually it strains everyone's vision and patience. That morning had been no different, and for long periods the quiet was punctuated only by occasional banter. Suddenly, Milt Butterworth, our photographer-videographer, broke the silence.

"Whoa . . . whoa . . . WHOA!"

The empty screen began to fill with dark shadows. Slowly, a definable image took shape, drifting eerily up from the bottom of the video screens. Then another voice—I can't remember whose—chimed in with "Oh, my God. . . ."

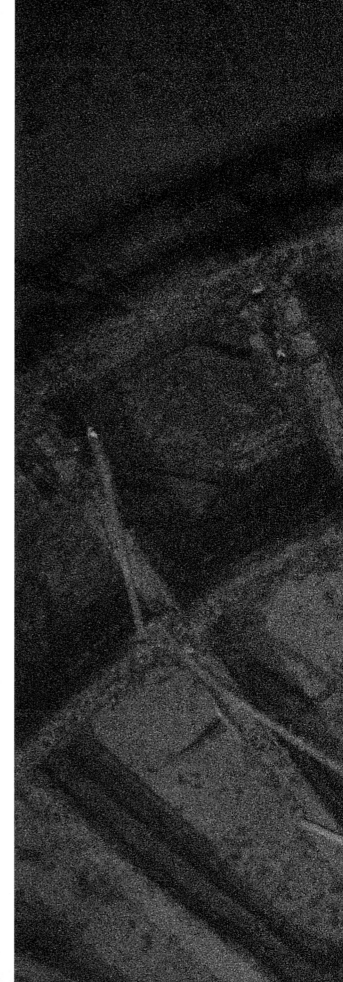

As *Nemo*'s cameras slid over the site, an unbelievable image scrolled by on the monitors: a rusting sidewheel lying flat in the eons-old mud. It was the one exceptionally distinguishing feature of the *Central America*. I was in awe.

Immediately, amid the shouts of everyone in the room, all thoughts of the previous site disappeared from our minds. We had come so close with the cameras that *Nemo*'s crew had to pull the robot up quickly to avoid striking the engine works, which protruded straight up.

"It was as if she was calling to us from a century ago," Bob said later. "Here I am, the *Central America*; you found me."

My thoughts immediately turned to the implications of our discovery. Corrosion experts were in disagreement over whether the sidewheels had survived; their existence would depend on the specific environment. I felt there was a good chance that this was indeed the *Central America*, but the sidewheel still represented only circumstantial evidence. After all, other sidewheel steamships had sunk over the years.

There were other issues to confront, as well. I did not want the news about our find to spread around the ship. Such information was, as always, imparted on a need-to-know basis, and only those in the control room needed to know. Business would go on as usual. I also had to consider when and how to communicate with partners and to analyze the logistics of investigating a new and unexpected site.

As it turned out, it wasn't until after many dives to explore and map the site and to recover incidental artifacts that *Nemo*'s main manipulator—known as "Dexter"—reached under the cowl of the ship's bell to lift it out of the mud. As sediment fell away in the slight current, we could clearly see an inscription. The words said: "MORGAN IRON WORKS—NEW YORK—1853." The identity of the ship was confirmed.

The *Central America*'s engine and ironworks had been installed at Morgan Iron Works in 1853. After 131 years of undisturbed slumber, the lost steamer had given up the secret of its final resting place. We had found one of the most legendary shipwrecks in American history.

*Recovery of the bronze ship's bell, which weighs about 275 pounds, provided definitive proof that the sunken vessel was indeed the* Central America.

*Right: An underwater photograph shows one of
Nemo's manipulator arms.*

*Inset: The Arctic Discoverer control room is the
operations center for the exploration and
recovery dives of Nemo. The crew here normally
consists of pilot, copilot, navigator,
videographer, and mission coordinator.*

Clockwise, from left: Nemo is lowered
from the deck of the research vessel
with coaxial fiber-optic cable
attached. Expedition members
monitor the dive while crewman
Bryan Anderson operates the crane.

*Nemo* **rests on the deck of the research vessel for several hours between dives.**

On the ocean bottom, the sturdy robot can withstand crushing deep-ocean pressure of 4,000 pounds per square inch (the equivalent of a car pressing on every inch of your body).

While a mission coordinator (often Bob Evans) manages the overall dive plan and the navigator monitors and controls the submersible's precise position over the shipwreck, the pilot directs specific recovery efforts. The copilot floods the ocean floor with powerful lights mounted on *Nemo's* various hinged booms. At the same time, Milt Butterworth, Columbus-America videographer, records every moment of undersea activity to obtain archaeological, historical, scientific, and numismatic data.

Recovery takes four basic forms. Gold dust and other loose material are gently sucked up into a small sea-vac, which retrieves all items too small for any other tool. Individual coins are recovered one by one with a suction-picker at the end of a flexible arm, while groups of coins, which have bonded naturally over time, are covered with silicone (later

*Below and right: Nemo is the world's first robot capable of extended work in the hostile environment of the deep ocean. At a depth of 8,000 feet and under more than 4,000 pounds of pressure, the submersible can maneuver with great dexterity, picking up an object as delicate as a drinking glass. The robot is equally proficient at moving objects weighing hundreds of pounds.*

removed) and collected en masse. Manipulator claws serve less delicate tasks, such as lifting heavy trunks and beams. Smaller items go into numbered slots in trays that slide into *Nemo's* drawers and compartments for the 90-minute trip back to the surface.

*Nemo* was designed to meet the multitude of demands recovery requires in a harsh environment. Tools can be adjusted in minute movements to improve the working angle, and the arms manipulate with absolute precision, making it possible to explore the shipwreck without knocking coins or artifacts into unreachable debris. The goal was to build in capabilities for heavy, delicate, and complex functions, using as many inexpensive, off-the-shelf materials as possible. This high-tech/low-tech approach helps reduce costs—important for a small, private operation such as this—and permits regular re-tooling for specific tasks.

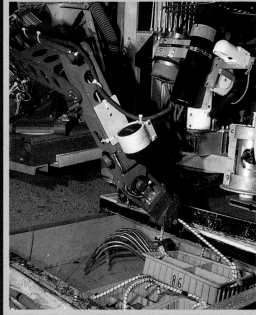

**Left and above:** Nemo *places collection trays on the ocean floor, preparing to collect. Each tray is clearly numbered to ensure correct logging. When filled, they are stored in a drawer in* Nemo *for the trip up to the research vessel.*

*Most of the expedition photographs were taken by photographer and videographer Milt Butterworth, here adjusting one of* Nemo's *cameras.*

*The manipulator arm is capable of precise movements that allow it to recover small objects.*

# CHAPTER FOUR
# GOLD DISCOVERED

The discovery of the *Central America* was an engineering success, and the shipwreck itself was a spectacular scientific discovery, but it was the gold that financed the expedition and that would allow us to stay and learn.

Predictably, the weather worsened by mid-October. Everyone was tired after long weeks at sea, and the pressure to get back to shore for the winter was intense. In the control room, our eyes began to play tricks on us as we searched the complex scene of rotting timbers, rusting iron, and general debris for something shiny or in the shape of an ingot.

Then, just days before we were to leave the site, Milt spotted some anomalies on some photographic negatives. One of the crew returned from the onboard lab, where he was developing some photographs. Bob, Barry, and I examined the images he was excited about and saw a color we had not encountered before: gold.

Because *Nemo*'s dives are precise, we knew exactly where on the shipwreck site the underwater robot had taken the pictures and where the next dive would take place. Within hours, the submersible was back on the bottom. As we flew the ROV toward the location of the photographs, Milt set the lights. At first we thought we were looking at bricks, but as the beams were adjusted, the color came out. Suddenly, the same monitors that had

*Overleaf: The enormous range of gold in the treasure includes coins and ingots as well as gold dust, flakes, and nuggets. A small sampling is shown here.*

*Left: Tommy Thompson holds a diminutive ingot. Opposite: In October 1988, Nemo's cameras revealed an amazing site: gold ingots strewn on the ocean floor like pickup sticks.*

revealed nothing but colorless ocean terrain for weeks now appeared to be painted a brilliant gold.

These weren't bricks, but ingots, ingots everywhere . . . stacked on the bottom like brownies . . . stacked like loaves of bread . . . spectacular gold bridges of gold ingots piled on top of timbers and spread over the ocean floor. Then, a little farther along, we found piles of coins, heaped in towers and seemingly spilling into frozen waterfalls. The coins in this part of the shipwreck, which we named the "Garden of Gold," were spread amid the wreckage, stretching beyond *Nemo*'s lights into the blackness of the sea.

We had all privately imagined the moment we would find the treasure, but none of us ever thought that it would be so otherworldly in its splendor. The gold of the *Central America* looked like something out of a fairy tale beyond one's wildest imagination. It sparkled with brilliance in the first light to play off its surface in 130 years.

The quantity alone was overwhelming, but as Milt brought the camera in for close-ups we found the condition even more astonishing. We could even read the dates on coins that seemed, unbelievably, as if they had left the mint the day before. As we stared at this unbelievable sight, it seemed impossible that the world that gave birth to this treasure was now gone forever. "It was as if the ship had just sunk moments before, not a century and a half ago," Milt recalled later. "The scene before us just telescoped time."

The tumult and the drama of the violent sinking, the slow wash of the sea, and the entropy of its surroundings had created a bizarre and fragile environment. It appeared inert, but we knew the ship's timbers and iron were being slowly

*Opposite: A pile of gold coins*
*($20 double eagles) is strewn on*
*timbers and coal at the shipwreck site.*

107

ravaged by the inexorable dance of the ages: degradation and decay. Yet amid this imperceptible drama of collapse, the gold rested like a timeless, unchanging centerpiece. A million years from now the wood would be consumed by bacteria, the iron rusted away, and most artifacts gone. Still glistening under a heavy blanket of sediment, the gold once buried amid this benthic chaos would be all that remained.

By the time we saw it, much of the gold had fallen into curious arrangements. Early on, *Nemo*'s cameras found a mysterious tower of 300 double eagle gold pieces standing alone unsupported. The coins had been cemented together by a light glaze of sea salts and rust, a miniature, golden, organic architecture resisting the constant push of gentle seafloor currents. We delighted in our early sightings. A range of early pioneer coins carried the distinctive marks of long-defunct assayers such as Moffat & Company and Wass, Molitor & Company—the lettering worn from jingling in the pockets of miners long dead. Coins were encrusted in the shape of wooden boxes that had rotted away or lay scattered as if they had only just settled quietly in the timbers.

In one place at the site, a remarkable cluster of eight gold coins (five double eagles, including one from the San Francisco Mint, and three eagles, mostly from private mints), a small gold ingot, and ten pieces of silver awaited

*Unaware of the enormous value of its perch, a brisingid sea star sits atop a stack of gold ingots.*

discovery. As in the coin tower, rust derived from the more than 750 tons of iron in the ship had bonded the mass together in the *Central America*'s alien environment. In the center of one side of this accretion, a rare $10 gold piece from the private mint of Dubosq and Co.—one of fewer than ten known examples—had fallen free many decades ago. Exotic ocean art.

Despite our exhilaration and wonder, a magnificent gravity—perhaps radiating from the beauty, the silence, and the timelessness of the scene—underscored the overpowering significance of the find. We knew we were looking at the wealth of early California, the hopes and dreams of true pioneers, a thousand stories of 19th-century America, and of tragedy and success.

We also knew that no other quantities of California gold still existed in original form. The gold we encountered was "priceless" not only because of its extraordinary intrinsic value but also because of its history and uniqueness. This was the very gold that drew people to California and fueled the nation's economy in the mid-19th century. It was the same gold that passengers cast onto the decks of the *Central America* in the panic of the storm and that bankers in New York had been awaiting so anxiously in September 1857. Part of our American heritage, this was history in the form of a national treasure. And we had found it.

*Left: Gold assay ingots, coins, and nuggets were recovered from the* **Central America.**

# The Gold of the *Central America*

T he shipwreck site of the *Central America* contains four types of gold: coins, assay ingots, individual nuggets that miners pulled directly from the ground and streams, and—amazingly—gold dust strewn amid the sediment. Each is characterized by extraordinary variety and texture and offers fascinating insight into the history of the fledgling and somewhat haphazard economy of San Francisco and Sacramento during the gold rush era.

*Tommy Thompson, at right, and Bob Evans hold tight to an enormous gold assay ingot, weighing more than 750 ounces, recovered from the shipwreck site.*

*The submersible is equipped with a vacuuming device, nicknamed "sea-vac," which is used to remove sediment and collect gold dust from Nemo's work area.*

# Dust and Nuggets

Dust and nuggets, which were among the most intriguing finds of the expedition, were the rawest form of gold coming out of the streams and gold fields in and around the foothills of the Sierra Nevada. Gold dust represented the base of San Francisco's earliest monetary system. Sending dust and raw nuggets all the way to the U.S. government's main mint in Philadelphia for assaying and coining was too costly and time consuming. Thus, San Francisco relied on a "dust economy," in which the gold dust, measured by weight or by the "pinch," served as currency.

This was a poor medium of exchange, however. For one thing, California gold dust varied from only 58 percent to more than 98 percent pure. Measurement was imprecise and prices highly speculative. At one point, the glut of dust in old San Francisco was so great that buyers were paying only $8.00 per ounce, far below the $20.67 U.S. government standard for pure gold and the roughly $18.00 per ounce paid by the Philadelphia Mint for gold dust.

Dust is collected when *Nemo's* sea-vac is used to clean up a specific work site on the ocean floor. It is necessary to sift through the sediment to extract the gold and small artifacts hidden within. After finding the first gleaming fleck, Bob regularly panned for gold dust.

It is ironic that this gold is twice-mined—once from California streams and again from 8,000 feet under the ocean surface in the 20th century. The nuggets are the most diverse gold pieces recovered. They are natural forms, like the dust, but intricate and far more unusual. Each one is unique, with the pieces ranging from just bigger than flecks of dust to fist-sized specimens of gold, quartz, and other minerals. Because the wealthy first-cabin passengers and the commercial shippers tended to carry their gold in ingots or coins, many of the nuggets on the *Central America* were almost certainly the prized possession of frugal miners traveling east in steerage class. For example, the Hearn brothers from Missouri, who took turns guarding their satchel of gold throughout the entire journey by steamship and train from San Francisco, and Joseph Bassford, who dropped his own while leaping into a lifeboat, are thought to have been carrying nuggets with them. Others who reportedly abandoned their wealth in despair just prior to the sinking were also in possession of gold in this form.

*This fascinating natural nugget of crystalline gold and milky quartz contains more than 13 ounces of gold.*

Bob Evans believed that the sediment at the shipwreck site might contain gold dust—which, in fact, it did. Samples were processed by the same method used by California miners: panning.

Above: Gold nuggets range from fist-sized clumps to tiny pieces that can fit on a fingertip.

Right: This natural gold nugget weighs 2.8 ounces.

115

# The Coins

The thousands of coins carried aboard the *Central America* in 1857 represent an illuminating cross-section of the minted currencies of the time. In addition to European and privately minted coins, passengers carried a modest amount of silver such as Mexican and Chilean pesos and Spanish pieces of four.

Such a wide range of currencies was not unusual. When James Marshall discovered gold at Sutter's Mill in 1848, California did not have a branch mint. As the population of San Francisco exploded from just a few hundred settlers to 25,000 gold-mad citizens in a matter of months, a monetary system couldn't be developed fast enough. Not surprisingly, entrepreneurs were among the first to fill the need for a dependable currency with privately minted coins. The oldest California gold coins found aboard the *Central America* were $10 gold pieces minted by Moffat & Company, one of the first and most esteemed of the early private coiners in California. A Philadelphian with a solid reputation in the assayer's trade, John Moffat, along with his three partners and his machinery set sail for the West Coast almost immediately upon the news of the gold rush. They carried with them various testimonials to their competence and integrity from the largest bullion dealers in the East, including that of the U.S. Secretary of the Treasury.

By August 1849, Moffat & Company was issuing $5 and $10 gold coins bearing a bust of Liberty, similar to the federal design but with the name "Moffat & Co." replacing the word "Liberty" on her coronet. On the other side soared an eagle, accompanied by the words "S.M.V. California Gold, 1849." The "S.M.V." stands for "Standard Mint Value."

Not all the assayers were as honest as Moffat & Company, and there were occasionally problems when some firms minted coins containing less than their stated amount or purity of gold. In frustration, the public turned to silver and to foreign coins on a limited basis.

Despite several well-publicized scandals, including the Baldwin & Company gold swindle of 1850, private coins continued to be accepted in the absence of public issue. Without a way to verify the purity of private coinage, however, a suspicious public increased the clamor for a branch mint that would issue "real coins," preferably in the $2.50, $5, and $10 denominations required for daily commerce. On September 30, 1850, the United States Congress established the U.S. Assay Office in San Francisco. This was not the full mint required to produce coins identical to U.S. mint issue, but at least it

*Above: The San Francisco Branch Mint was established in 1854. Right: Gold coins rest in their eerie underwater vault.*

could mint provisional coins from the local alloy. Augustus Humbert, a watchmaker from New York City, was named U.S. Assayer; Moffat and Company received the contract.

Unfortunately, the U.S. government failed to address the critical need for small commercial denominations and did not authorize any that were lower than $50. The most commonly used government denomination, Humbert's $50 octagonal "slug," was wildly unpopular. However, the words "Augustus Humbert United States Assayer of Gold 1851" enscripted around the eight edges to discourage shaving made it "tamper evident," and the coin did succeed in driving many of the debased private issues off the street.

But even this was a mixed blessing. The disappearance of these privately minted coins made the smaller denominations even scarcer and depressed commerce. Although it was the proper weight and purity, the $50 slug became so undesirable that it eventually traded at a discount of $48, which was no improvement over the earlier debased coinage.

Samuel Wass and Agoston Molitor, Hungarian refugees and graduates of the esteemed School of the Mines in Germany, capitalized on the $50 slug's unpopularity when they opened a gold processing

*This 1851 $50 gold piece is from Augustus Humbert, the United States Assayer of Gold in San Francisco.*

plant and assay office in San Francisco in October 1851. Wass, Molitor & Company began to issue round $10 and $20 coins. During a later coinage crisis, in 1855, the company produced the only circulating $50 coin ever minted in California. An example appeared in one of the very first trays of coins *Nemo* brought to the surface. The wide acceptance of all the Hungarian assayers' issue is evident by the many other Wass Molitor coins that were possessed by the *Central America* passengers.

In February 1852, the government finally authorized the issue of $5 and $10 coins. Thr Moffat had sold his interest in the company but his partners, Curtis, Perry and Ward, won the contract and produced many of the $10 eagles so plentiful in the treasure. They also produced half eagles and double eagles. When the lesser denominations began to appear in the market, the $50 slug regained public favor because it was useful for large purchases. Its unique octagonal shape became a symbol of California coinage, and several of the slugs found their way on board the *Central America.* By 1854, the government established a full-fledged U.S. Mint offering coins struck from California gold. As the common currency of the day, thousands of these government-issued coins were carried by passengers as well

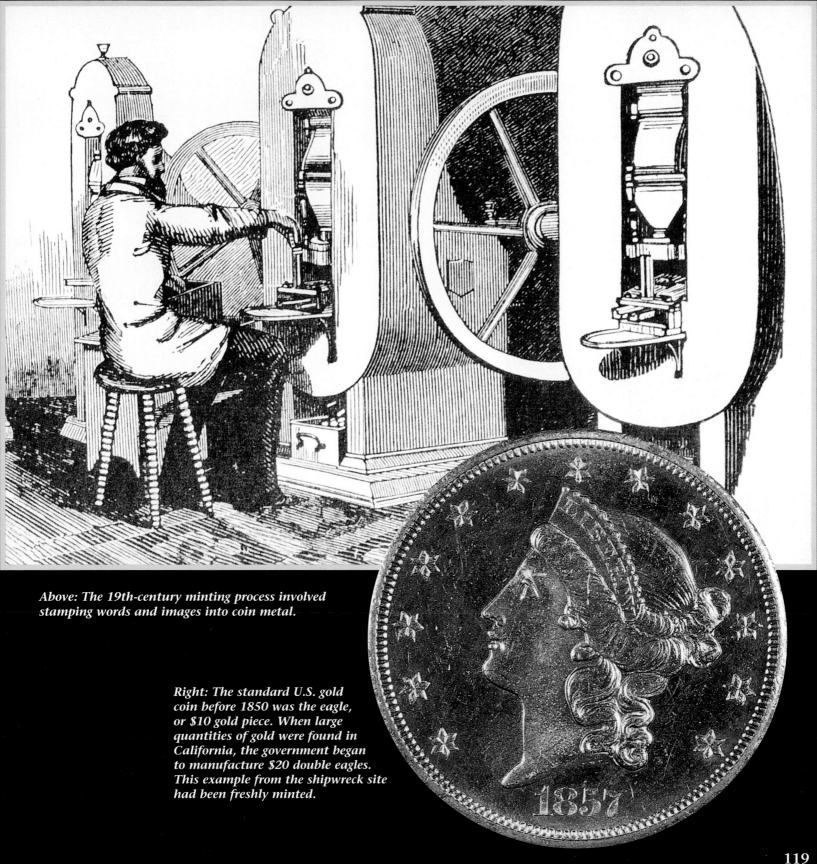

*Above: The 19th-century minting process involved stamping words and images into coin metal.*

*Right: The standard U.S. gold coin before 1850 was the eagle, or $10 gold piece. When large quantities of gold were found in California, the government began to manufacture $20 double eagles. This example from the shipwreck site had been freshly minted.*

*Left: This $50 gold coin was produced by Wass, Molitor, and Co., a private coiner active in 1850s California.*

*Above: Coins made at the U.S. government's San Francisco Branch Mint were found in spectacular condition, as if they were freshly struck.*

*Right: Gold coins range in value from the tiny octagonal 25-cent pieces up to $50 pieces, which each contain 2 1/2 ounces of gold.*

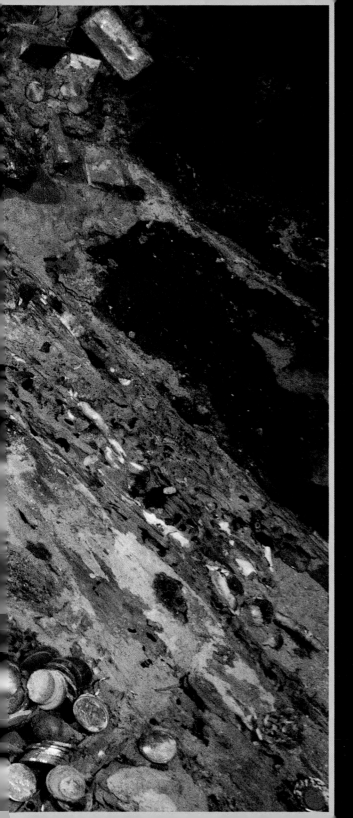

*Above: A large deposit of assay ingots we[...] found at the shipwreck site.*

*Far left: This portion of the "Garden of Gold" deposit shows all the forms in which the shipwreck gold occurs: coins, ingots, nuggets, and dust.*

*Left: Nemo's precision arm reaches out to delicately explore and excavate.*

# Ingots

Despite the near-mint-state condition of a wide variety of rare coins, the most unusual element of the *Central America* treasure may be the hundreds of "assay ingots." These range from pocket-sized, such as the small, rectangular five-ounce Blake & Company ingots produced in Sacramento, to a massive, 63-pound, "two by four" (2 by 4 by 11 1/2-inch) ingot from Justh and Hunter. Their purity varies as widely as their size, differing from 580 fine (just over half gold), to 973 fine (indicating a nearly pure gold value).

Although less common in the consumer market-place than the coins, the ingots are as revealing of the era and are also more unusual in that they are all private issue. Many began as dust and nuggets in the pockets of miners, who brought the raw gold to private assayers for weighing and valuation. The assayers melted down the gold, molded it into ingots, then shaved off a corner for their commission and to measure purity. Finally they would stamp the gold with unique identifying marks, indicating the weight, purity, and value, as well as their own maker's marks, and return the ingots to the owners. Gold in this form was the preferred type shipped to banks and other

*Opposite: Assay ingots are a diverse and unusual component of the Central America treasure.*

*Above: The minting process involves "running," or pouring, molten gold and molding it into ingots.*

Assay ingots from
five companies
were found.

businesses, as well as to the U.S. government.
Commercial shippers also brought their gold to private assayers, but did so in larger allotments.

Five assayers are represented in the treasure of the
*Central America*: Blake and Company, founded by
Gorham Blake, a Sacramento assayer; Kellogg &

Humbert (Augustus Humbert was the watchmaker and
original U.S. Assayer); Justh and Hunter (formed by E.
Justh, a former employee of the San Francisco Mint);
Harris, Marchand & Company, a well-known firm of
the day; and Henry Henstch, a San Francisco banker.

126

**KELLOGG & HUMBERT**
**ASSAYERS,**
No. 108 MONTGOMERY STREET,
SAN FRANCISCO.

*Above: An advertisement gives the San Francisco
address of Kellogg & Humbert, Assayers.*

*Above right: A depression formed in the middle
of an ingot as the gold cooled and hardened.*

*Right: A variety
of ingots shows
the mark of
Kellogg &
Humbert.*

*Above and right: Small ingots such as these were nicknamed "brownies" by the recovery team. These ingots are approximately one to three inches long.*

*Right: An ingot shows the marks of the San Francisco office of assayer Kellogg & Humbert.*

*Above: Rust deposits add beautiful coloration to this ingot from Harris, Marchand & Company.*

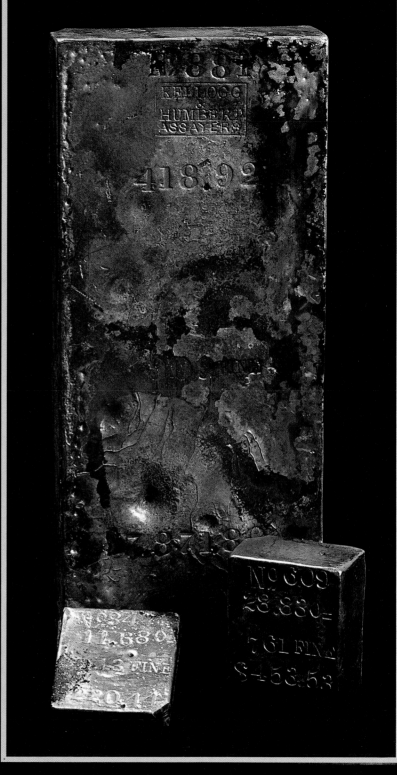

*Above: A brick-sized ingot from Kellogg & Humbert stands next to two "brownies."*

*Above:* Nemo's suction cup device picks up individual gold coins, one at a time.

*Right:* Artifacts, gold, and scientific specimens from the shipwreck are carefully collected and placed in a retractable drawer within Nemo for transport to the surface.

# Meticulous Recovery

rom the earliest planning stages of *Nemo*, meticulous recovery has been the guiding principle of the *Central America* project. Working around the fallen timbers and tons of iron of a historic wooden shipwreck requires the ability to perform heavy work—lifting and moving unwieldy materials and managing complex, multilayered excavation areas. Recovering coins and ingots from this complex environment also requires great delicacy and surgical precision. Valuable coins, for example, must be handled, often individually, with utmost care to preserve their exact condition and to avoid disturbing the rest of the deposit.

*Nemo* recovers large ingots with padded fingers, but the robot recovers individual coins with a suction-picker. Using the 3-D monitor aboard the research vessel a mile and a half above to gauge distances to fractions of an inch, *Nemo*'s operator carefully manipulates this device as close to the surface of a coin as possible and then activates the suction to hold the coin against a rubber cup. He then guides *Nemo*'s arm to carry the coin to a nearby tray, and releases it into a numbered slot. Sitting nearby in the RV control room, the videographer records the entire process while the dive coordinator logs in the time and the number of the coin. Once the tray is filled, *Nemo* places it inside its retractable storage drawer for the trip to the surface.

When coins are clustered together, the pilot follows a different procedure, using *Nemo* to surround the

*Using the suction picker,* Nemo *carefully places each coin in a separate numbered compartment in a collection tray.*

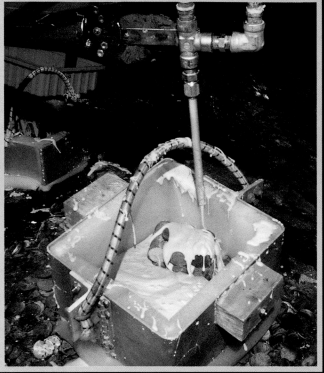

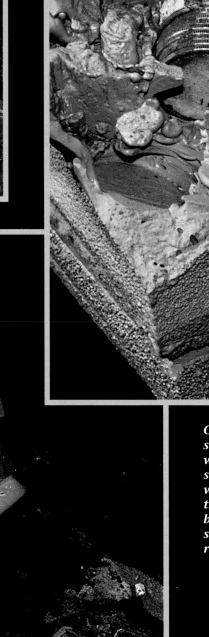

*Clockwise, from left: A padded mold is used to surround a stack of coins. The mold is then injected with a fluid silicone compound that congeals in several hours so that the block can be recovered without disrupting the arrangement. Once it sets, the compound becomes a flexible rubber that can be easily peeled away; encased in this block of silicone, approximately 300 gold coins were recovered from the Central America.*

*Opposite: As the trays are unpacked, the coins are laid out in a pattern identical to that of the numbered slots in the collection trays. This is one step in the identification process that allows the material to be traced back to its location on the bottom.*

cluster with a padded frame, which is then filled with a special silicone gel. Thus held fast, the coins are brought to the surface. The congealed silicone is later peeled away, releasing the individual coins.

When *Nemo* surfaces with the gold, the collection trays go to the ship's lab. There team members are able to examine the coins and ingots closely, catalogue them in detail, and store them for transport back to labs on shore. Coins are usually protected in the plastic sleeves used by numismatists, although stable clusters are sometimes left encased in their silicone. Individual containers hold ingots, which are carefully wrapped in cloth.

The dust and nuggets suctioned up from the ocean floor by the sea-vac are panned from the sediment and placed in numbered vials.

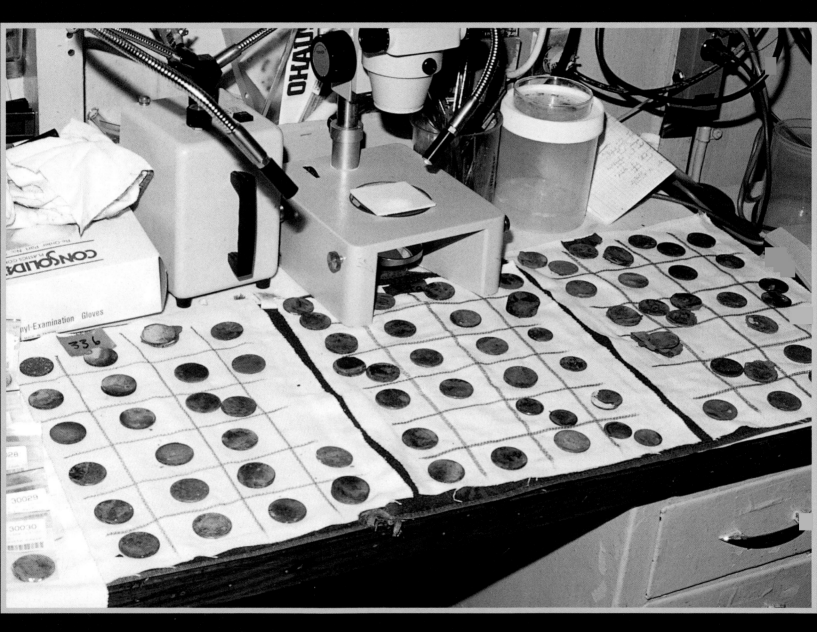

# CHAPTER FIVE
# TIME CAPSULES

The treasure of the *Central America* consists of far more than gold. The real windfall is the knowledge the ship has provided us, not only about the deep ocean and sea life but also about life in mid-19th-century America. In the cabins and steerage compartments, and packed in the hold, were thousands of personal possessions. One hundred fifty-three of the passengers and crew survived the storm, but virtually everything aboard with them—the gold cuff links, the favorite teak hairbrush, the miners' tools, the soft leather boots, the half-written letter—was claimed by a greedy sea. While apparently ordinary, these trappings of daily existence have enormous value, offering insight into travel customs, clothing styles, and social and cultural customs of the 1850s, along with preferences in everything from tobacco to literature.

All are reminders of lives saved and lost, and of stories we may never know. While *Nemo* was gently blowing sediment away from some timbers, for example, we found our gaze returned by the haunting stare of a young man in an ambrotype, an early type of photograph. Bowls and pitchers from the passenger cabins and cups and dishes from the galley are also eerie links to the past. Many of these ceramic objects survived exposure in the marine environment with little evidence of change. And while items containing iron and copper show considerable corrosion, the debris field is still rich with many types of artifacts awaiting discovery.

The many intact passenger trunks at the site are a particular reminder of the diverse individuals who sailed aboard the *Central America*. A time capsule created by tragedy a century and a half earlier, each piece of luggage reveals the types of belongings a traveler packed for a long journey in the mid-1800s. We know that the lack of air and light, the frigid temperature, and even the compression of the packing itself create an almost perfect microenvironment for preservation of the contents.

We decided to recover the first trunk after having observed it at the shipwreck site for years. We knew it came from the *Central America*, but would the

*This ambrotype from the Easton trunk was wrapped in a sealed package that included a note reading, "Good morning Sir, do you know me?" So far, relatives and descendants of the Eastons have been unable to identify this young man.*

*Overleaf: A leather-bound passenger trunk, foreground, lies next to a capstan.*

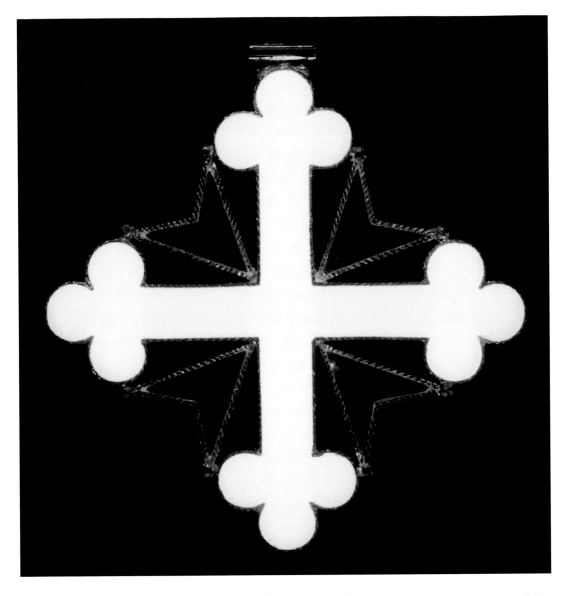

*During several dives in 1988, Nemo's cameras caught sight of a small cross lying on the sea floor. It proved to be enamel-covered gold and was apparently part of a medal. In June 1992, a researcher learned that this find represents The Order of St. Maurice and St. Lazarus, which was founded in Italy in 1434 and is now defunct. The medal was conferred by the king of Italy on individuals distinguished in art, science, letters, public and military service, and charitable work. Expedition researchers have not yet identified the recipient, but it is known that there were four Italians among the Central America's passengers.*

contents be recognizable? Once the piece of luggage was transported to Columbus, preliminary examination of the very top layer revealed that the items surviving in the black water inside were intact. A group of scientists, historians, videographers, technicians, and graduate students was soon gathered at The Ohio State University to record every minute of the painstaking three-day unpacking process.

Under the direction of Dr. Kathryn Jakes, a polymer chemist from the College of Human Ecology at Ohio State, and Bob Evans of the Columbus-America Discovery Group, research team members began to gently lift out items one by one—something like peeling away the skin of a large, rectangular black onion.

The team was also joined by the late Dr. Lucy Sibley, an Ohio State textile historian, and Charles Kleibacker, designer-in-residence at the college's Historic Costume and Textile Collection. As the group's work progressed, researchers carefully unfolded or unrolled each piece of clothing for preliminary analysis and cataloging. Arranged on a screen, each was then quick-frozen and slowly dried to protect the water-logged materials.

*This trunk was discovered in the debris field of the* Central America *in October 1990. Its original owners were passengers Ansel and Adeline Easton, who were on their honeymoon.*

Throughout this intricate excavation, an almost reverential atmosphere prevailed. Even though it was more than a century after the trunk had been packed, we all felt a strange immediacy as we looked through someone else's belongings, and particularly as we began to learn more about the owners. We knew, of course, that their trunk—this trunk—had been packed in gold rush San Francisco in 1857. And because we had found examples of both men's and women's clothing, we felt sure it belonged to a couple. Our imaginations had no difficulty in adding details. Given the customs of the day, it was likely the wife who did the packing, perhaps while humming "Oh, Susannah" in a chintz-decorated bedroom. Had she been thinking about her upcoming trip while carefully folding the pretty print robe or her husband's elegant dress shirts? Had she been excited about going east? Or apprehensive? Clearly she could not have anticipated the nightmare that awaited, or that her trunk would next be opened and the clothes next unfolded a century later and half a continent away by scientists and historians.

Our research told us that this woman had not drowned because all the female passengers aboard the *Central America* survived. But had her husband lived? Or

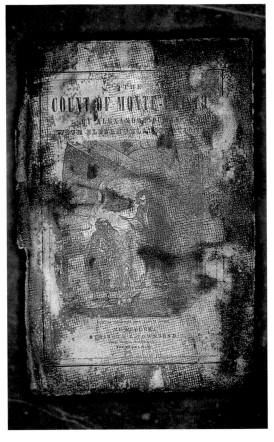

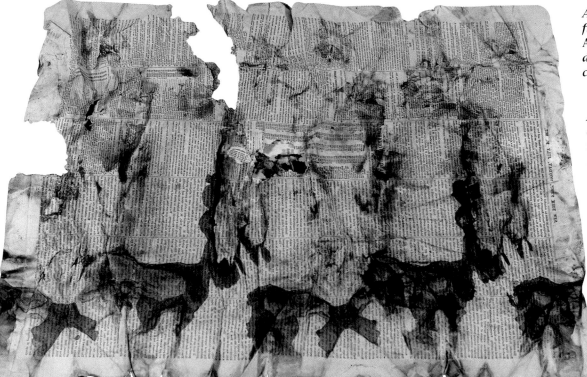

*Above right: Among the most important finds in the wreckage of the Central America are the handwritten and printed documents, still legible and in remarkable condition after 133 years in the deep ocean.*

*Above left and left: When this copy of the New York News was unrolled, it was found to contain a man's dress shirt belonging to tycoon William Ralston, who later founded the Bank of California with Adeline Easton's brother, Darius Ogden Mills. As a favor, the Eastons may have been taking Ralston's shirt to be copied by a tailor in New York.*

Columbus-America's *chief scientist, Bob Evans, inspects the Easton trunk as it is being removed from its container and readied for excavation.*

# The Easton Trunk

The first trunk recovered belonged to newlyweds Ansel Ives Easton and Adeline Mills Easton, who were separated when the ship was sinking. Adeline was among those transferred to the brig *Marine* but her husband was cast on the waves when the *Central America* went down. Although Adeline had no way of knowing it, Ansel was fortunate enough to be among those rescued by the bark *Ellen*. Six days later the honeymooners were reunited in Norfolk, Virginia.

Ansel was a San Francisco entrepreneur and Adeline was the sister of Darius Ogden Mills, later a cofounder of the Bank of California. The couple later had two children, Ansel Mills Easton and Jennie Ellen Marine Easton. Jennie was named after the two rescue ships that had saved her

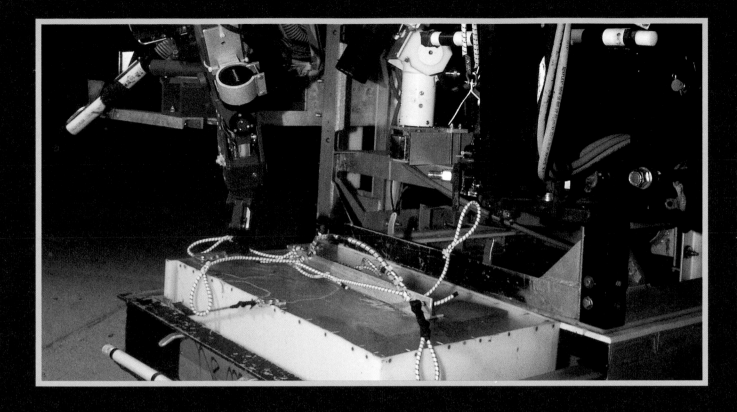

*Team members constructed a special container to hold the Easton trunk during its long journey to the surface. In this photo, Nemo's manipulator is engaged in the delicate operation of tying cords that helped secure the container to the submersible.*

*A technician inspects the trunk on the deck of the Arctic Discoverer.*

141

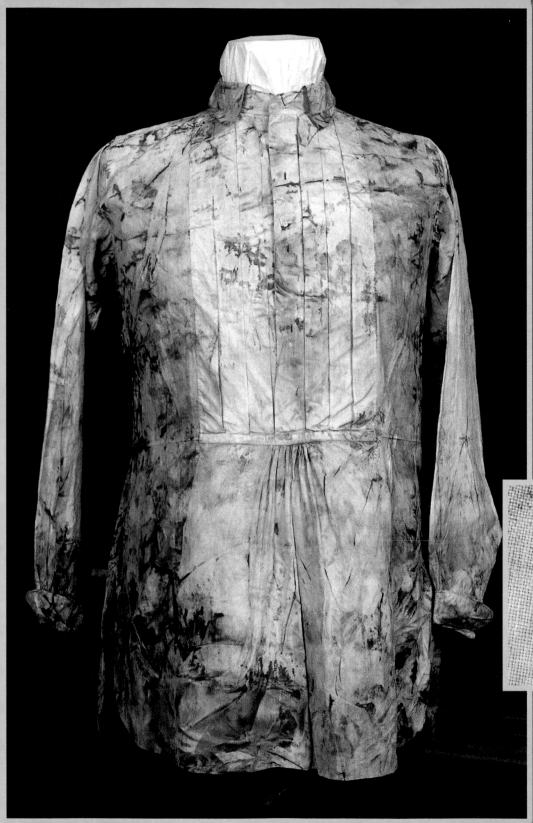

A dog's-head watch fob, with garnet eyes, was among the jewelry found.

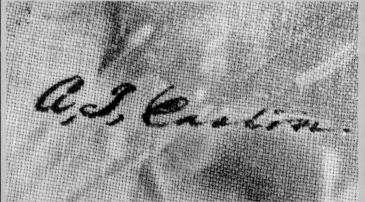

Left and above: A name marked on one of the fancy dress shirts revealed the identity of its owner: Ansel Ives Easton. Ansel's dress shirts are made of linen. They are finely sewn, custom-made garments.

A pair of Derringer pistols (invented by 19th-century American gunsmith Henry Derringer) from the trunk is a reminder that Easton lived in an age when men regularly carried guns.

Ansel Easton's single-breasted waistcoat is made with patterned silk in the front sections.

Left: A gunpowder flask with an embossed eagle is shown with its top.

Right: Another recovered watch fob is made of gold and quartz.

*During the 19th century it was common for a gentleman to give a lady a ring like this as a token of affection. It is known as a "regard ring," because the first letters of the names of the stones—ruby (missing in this ring), emerald, garnet, amethyst, rose quartz, and diamond—spell out the word "regard." This piece of jewelry presents a romantic mystery. Who was the lady who owned the ring, and who was the gentleman who gave it to her?*

was she tragically widowed just a couple of weeks after packing these clothes? Who were these people?

In the mood of quiet awe that linked us with this unknown pair, a picture began to emerge when we examined their personal possessions. In addition to such clothing as a lace-trimmed dressing gown, vests for day and evening wear, and a man's shirt—curiously rolled in a newspaper—we found a handsome dog's-head watch fob with garnet eyes, a small Chinese carving, and various toiletries, including a hairbrush with hair clinging to the bristles. Because the clothing was well made, we knew the owners were well-to-do and were probably first-cabin passengers. Clothing size shows they were small in stature, while books and correspondence suggest they were readers and letter-writers.

We had a great surprise when we found the handwritten inscription, "A. I. Easton," on one of the finely stitched men's dress shirts. It was incredible luck. Of all the people on board the *Central America*, the Eastons were among those we knew most about. Finding their trunk right away gave us a leg up in piecing together the historical evidence. Addie's letter about the sinking had been among the most useful of the passenger accounts, and now we had located an entire trunk belonging to the same survivor.

A second trunk offered further opportunities for discovery. Inside we found several sets of men's clothes. Among these were a half-dozen completely new woolen undershirts and pairs of socks, some bearing the mark "super merino."

Once again, a faint portrait of the mystery traveler began to emerge as more contents came to light: a remarkably preserved cache of cigars and chunks of tobacco, a shaving kit, and three books—*The Count of Monte Cristo, Prairie Flower,* and *Lady Lee's Widowhood,* a sample of some light fiction of the day. Months later, after the freeze-dry process allowed careful unfolding, we were able to read a letter from the trunk. Finally, the owner was revealed. "Allow me to introduce to you Mr. John Dement of Oregon City," an Oregon merchant

had written. "Mr. Dement is one of our largest merchants here. . . . I have given him this hoping that you would introduce him to such of my friends as may be in Baltimore while he is there. . . ."

*The second trunk retrieved from the* Central America's *debris field belonged to Oregon pioneer John Daniel Dement.*

It was almost as if Dement were being introduced to us from across the years. John Dement was one of the last two people rescued by the *Ellen* on September 13, 1857. He spent 12 hours in the water and was saved only because Ansel Easton, rescued shortly before Dement, convinced the bark's captain to make one more tack in an effort to save his friend Robert T. Brown.

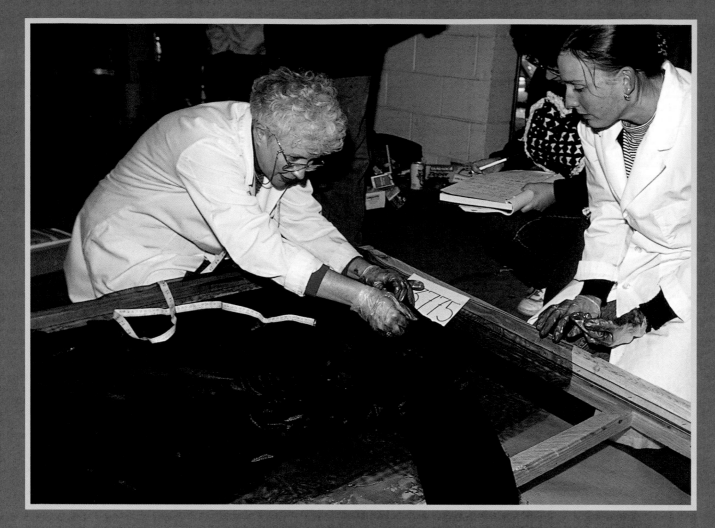

# Historical Textiles Research

The recovery of clothing inside passenger trunks from the *Central America* shipwreck site presents rare opportunities for historical studies and scientific research. Professors and students from the Department of Consumer and Textile Sciences in the College of Human Ecology at Ohio State have joined the recovery and research effort and pursue their efforts with the same exacting care characterizing all expedition projects.

To avoid any change in their environment, *Nemo* begins the collection process by placing the trunks in translucent, water-filled containers on the ocean floor. These same vats are transported to labs at Ohio State,

where each garment and paper artifact is removed from the trunks and unfolded or unrolled in demineralized water while resting on a supporting screen.

Lifted from the water, the screens and textiles then go in a freezer at 19 degrees below zero Fahrenheit so they can dry slowly during a period of three to four weeks. The next step is careful study of the dry garments in a climate-controlled laboratory. This involves recording structure and dimension and examining the chemical and physical changes in the flax, cotton, wool, and silk fibers that occurred while the materials were on the ocean floor. Microscopic views, for example, provide evidence of the

*Above: Textile historian Dr. Lucy Sibley, left, and textile scientist Dr. Kathryn Jakes examine a silk necktie from the Easton trunk.*

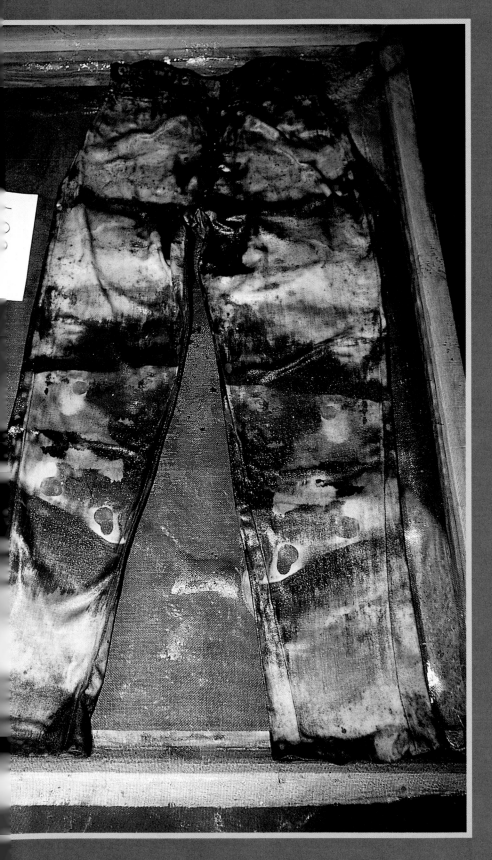

*Left: As garments are removed from the trunks, they are carefully unrolled or unfolded on specially constructed frames over which sheets of fiberglass screening are stretched. John Dement's five-button-fly pants of white linen await examination by textile scientists and historians.*

deterioration caused by micro-organisms. Once the garments are stabilized, clothing historians then bring their own expertise to the process. These professionals study the fashion styles and how the garments were made. That information not only tells us about clothing in the 1850s but also about what people packed for a sea voyage.

Buying patterns of the day are revealed as well. Undershirts and socks from the Easton trunk were ready-made, for example, but many of the couple's clothes appear to have been custom-designed. Little did the tailors realize that some 130 years later, someone would be examining their handiwork.

147

*Above: This is Adeline Easton's linen morning robe, which has just been laid on a screen. This type of dress was worn at home during the morning hours to receive guests, but would not be worn on the street.*

*Left: Microscopic examination provides insight into how the deep-ocean environment both preserves and degrades fabrics.*

*Dr. Kathryn A. Jakes, a polymer chemist and textile scientist at The Ohio State University's Department of Consumer and Textile Sciences, carefully removes a garment from the Dement trunk.*

*The Easton trunk contained two of Adeline's morning robes. This plain-woven cotton example is one of only a few garments recovered that were made of a printed fabric.*

149

When they miraculously found Brown clinging to debris, Dement was with him. An article published after the *Central America* tragedy described Dement as "a muscular, well-built man . . . with strong nerves, and apparently . . . capable of retaining his presence of mind in emergencies."

*A humorous popular novel,* Lady Lee's Widowhood, *by General Sir E. B. Hamley, was packed in the Dement trunk.*

While we made unexpected discoveries, we also know of numerous items that were on the ship but that have not yet been found. For instance, one steerage passenger, John O. Stevens, was carrying 200 sketches and paintings by naturalist John Woodhouse Audubon (1812–1862). If they were stored in a trunk that survived intact, it is likely that this invaluable piece of Americana is recoverable.

What we *have* discovered so far offers an extraordinary opportunity to study samples that have been preserved in the deep ocean. Dr. Jakes points out that few textiles have ever been recovered from a marine environment. Those from the *Central America* provide us with the opportunity to learn what happens to textiles and paper fibers on the ocean floor over a long period. She and her students at Ohio State have subjected microsamples of the fabrics, taken from inner seams and other unobtrusive areas, to chemical and physical tests to study their condition and determine the appropriate procedures for handling waterlogged historic textiles. The scientific study reveals how different materials degrade under different circumstances and provides data about the chemical processes that work on them in the deep ocean.

*Paper conservation expert Harry Campbell from The Ohio State University works on a small book from the Dement trunk. Observing and assisting are Columbus-America's Debbie Willaman and Bob Evans.*

Study of the recovered objects and experiments the scientists have initiated will add to our growing body of knowledge about how to recover responsibly and preserve all types of materials from the deep ocean. Dr. Jakes, for example, has placed a number of fabric samples at the shipwreck site to compare degradation of various materials during specific time periods.

At the same time, historians study the materials in a social and cultural context to gain insight into day-to-day life in mid-19th-century America. While Ansel Easton wore custom-made clothes and fashionable dress for a man of the period, for example, John Dement's trunk contained work clothes, such as loose sack coats that were patched and torn. Their construction indicates that he was able to purchase commercially manufactured clothes in the Oregon Territory, a point of interest since the ready-to-wear apparel industry was in its infancy in the 1850s. It is also revealing to learn that buttons on one of his waistcoats carry a regimental insignia and were probably transferred from clothing he wore as a soldier in the Mexican-American War.

*Above: The faint image of a man is still visible in this ambrotype recovered from the shipwreck.*

*Left: An assortment of bottles, probably once containing beer and wine, rests on the sediment in the debris field. A number of ambrotype photo plates can be seen to the left. The presence of so many of these in one location suggests a professional photographer was among the passengers.*

153

One of our most pleasant surprises came with the paper items found on the shipwreck. Scientists had long speculated that the frigid temperature and lack of light in deep water might preserve such materials. Moreover, the anaerobic microenvironment occurring in a sealed trunk subject to deep-water pressure could also help preserve fragile paper items. The newspaper wrapped around the shirt in the Eastons' trunk, books and journals, John Dement's letter of introduction, and even his checkbook, which we also discovered, confirmed scientists' highest hopes. Perhaps in the future even ancient manuscripts might be recovered in readable condition from other deep-water shipwrecks.

That kind of understanding, along with the technology that allows us to work in the deep ocean, should provide incentive for seeking other treasures previously considered inaccessible and clues to the secrets that can be learned about the past from study of the ocean depths. For now, work continues on this American treasure and on the mysteries it continues to reveal.

# Artifact Recovery

*A*mong *Nemo*'s ingenious fittings are divided plastic trays with up to 24 compartments that enable the robot to recover artifacts from the shipwreck systematically and efficiently. To keep track of every object retrieved, each tray—and each compartment— receives a number. As the robot picks up artifacts from the shipwreck, they are also given identification numbers and logged into a computer system. An object's location on the site at the time of recovery is electronically recorded, along with the identification numbers of the tray and compartment holding it. Once the trays are on the RV *Arctic Discoverer*, each artifact is removed from its compartment, tagged with its computer-generated number, cataloged, and stored in a way appropriate for the material.

*Top and right: Among the items recovered in a tray is a blue glass goblet showing traces of red or pink paint, which must have emphasized the design.*

*Center: This passenger trunk has disintegrated after 135 years on the ocean floor. The two two-foot rods in the foreground were placed at the site to help determine the size of objects.*

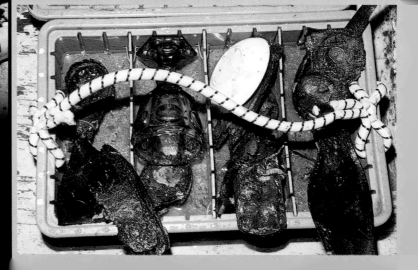

*Above: A brown stoneware bottle shows traces of the deep-ocean worms that had made a home on it.*

*Left: A selection of bottles includes the "CAM" flask at top, so-called by researchers because of three initials embossed on the glass. Could this have belonged to third officer Charles A. Meyers?*

After recovering the large ship's bell, researchers were delighted to discover another in the debris field. The second bell, however, proved to be much smaller—about six inches high. It is probably a signal or dinner bell.

Above: Researchers were charmed by the small molded face on this ceramic container. The tube was left behind by a deep-ocean worm.

Right: This whale-oil lamp still retained the scent of oil.

"As the night grew darker rockets of distress were set off. Blankets and rugs were packed about the smoke-stacks and hatches to keep out the water, but to no avail. 'We are righting,' I said as we watched the lamps with great interest to see them hang gradually level. I tried to cheer those near me with that thought, little knowing that as the ship became waterlogged she would right herself before sinking."
—Adeline Mills Easton, first-cabin passenger
(Story of Our Wedding Journey, 1911).

The tiny size of this ironstone mug implies that it is a toy, but its sturdy construction seems to indicate it was meant for everyday use by a child.

*"My husband said that he did not care about himself, if it were possible that I could be saved, and the little child."*
—Mary Swan, steerage passenger (The New-York Times, September 21, 1857)

This delicate pitcher was probably used to hold cream or milk.

Above: A ceramic jar lid from a jar of shaving cream made by Eugene Roussel of Philadelphia.

Right: Another ceramic lid came from a container of "Highly Perfumed Bear's Grease," a hair-care product made by X. Bazin, also of Philadelphia. In a strange coincidence, the two decorated cosmetic jars—the only examples recovered from the shipwreck—were manufactured by successive occupants of the exact same address.

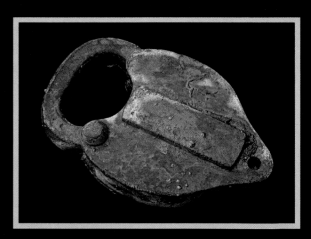

This padlock was recovered on the site.

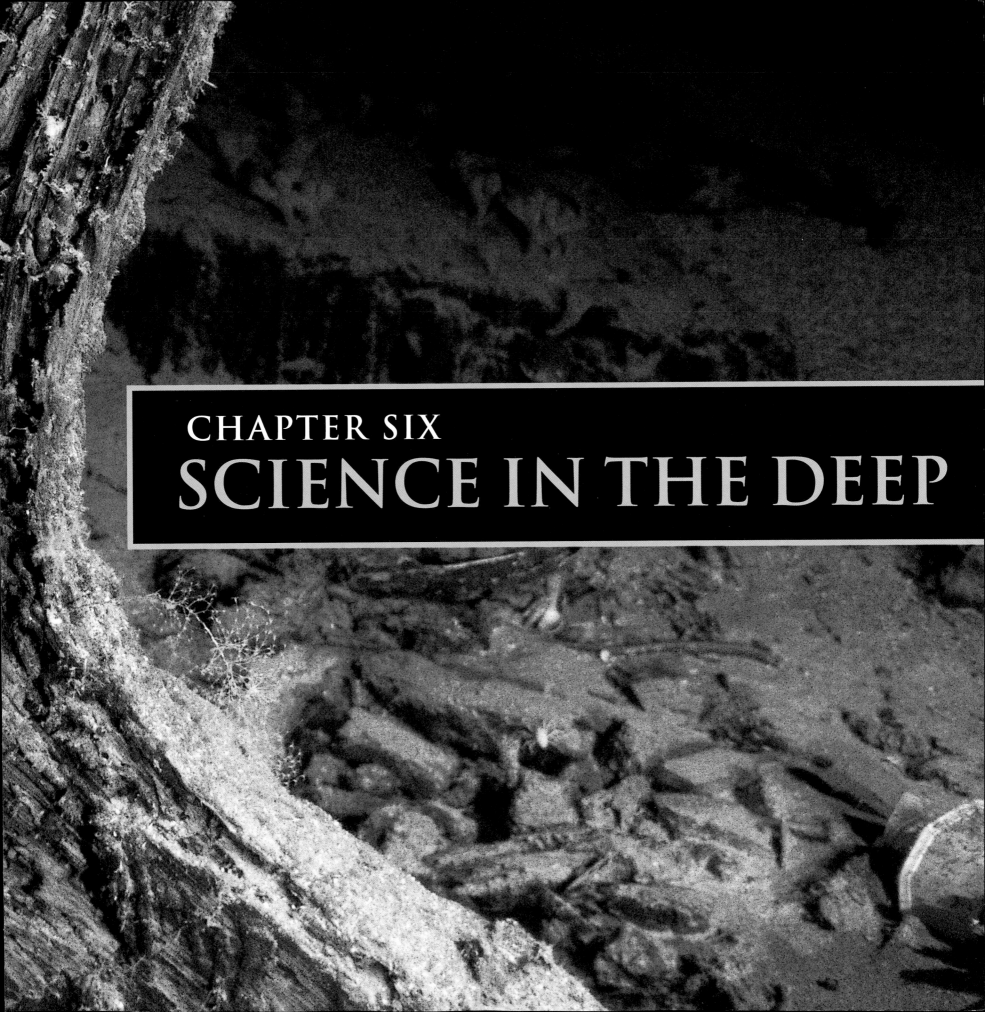

# CHAPTER SIX
# SCIENCE IN THE DEEP

The gold shines through the blackness as a slow, life-giving dance begins in the void. A delicate white starfish, a diminutive male, clings precipitously, incongruously to a tower of 300 double eagle gold pieces minted a century ago and a continent away. Slowly, a large, reddish female starfish inches over and places her central disk over the male's. Three days later, carrying new life, she scuttles off the million-dollar trysting place to look for sustenance amid the rotting timbers and rusting iron nearby.

Except for this lonely oasis, the sea floor appears as one of the most forbidding and desolate underwater deserts on earth—a vast and watery expanse unbroken by significant animal or plant life. Here, in this black and frigid sea, the waterfalls of coins, rivers of ingots, and blankets of gold dust glitter under the lights of *Nemo*. Despite its grandeur, the gold is a mere accent for the vermilion starfish, translucent glass sponges, pink and gold coral, yellow sea anemones, purple sea cucumbers, orange crabs, and even the gray eels and sharks that have established a colony around the lost ship. This paradise of color is more than a mariner's Elysium in a bleak setting; it is a biological mystery whose very existence scientists are struggling to understand.

Indeed, no one anticipated that life would flourish on this featureless undersea plain in the Atlantic Ocean known as the Blake Ridge. Two hundred miles east of the Carolinas and 8,000 feet down, the ridge is the last of the continental shelf's several sloping steps before the deepest level of ocean floor, at 17,000 feet. The "sand" of the desertlike seabed here consists not of quartz, found in common beach sand, but of microscopic shells of tiny dead mollusks, sea butterflies, and protozoans that have been raining down from the surface for eons. Accumulating at a rate of less than one inch every 1,000 years, the sediment has also begun to coat the shipwreck with a translucent white veil undisturbed by the warm and vigorous wash of the Gulf Stream above. Only the occasional benthic (ocean-bottom) storm of two to three knots stirs the depths.

*Overleaf: A hanging knee, which once braced the deck of the* Central America, *now serves as a perch for feathery golden corals, reddish-purple soft corals, an orange brisingid sea star, and a sea anemone. Wood-boring bivalves have riddled the knee with holes.*

*Opposite: A colony of perhaps 50 graceful brisingid sea stars lives on one of the sidewheels, and are also found at many other places on the site. Only females appear to be orange in color; males are much smaller and white. Brisingids typically have 10 to 14 arms, which they release if they are threatened. Within several months they can grow replacements.*

*Pteropod ooze forms the bulk of the sediment in the vicinity of the shipwreck. Scientists have discovered that it takes about a thousand years to build up less than one inch.*

The first indication of sea life came just before *Nemo*'s cameras approached the *Central America*'s sidewheel, when a series of tiny, mysterious whorls appeared on the otherwise monotonous bottom. The whorls turned out to be trails of sea cucumbers and other invertebrates. Months of bottom time and thousands of hours of video revealed that the *Central America* had been transformed into a vibrant reef for a diverse community of sea creatures. Together, the timbers, iron, and scattered gold serve as home and feeding ground to a range of organisms—including invertebrates that have attached to the debris—and provide protective cover for prey and predator alike.

*Left: Tommy Thompson, left, explains the function of* Nemo's *precision arm to Dr. Ron Toll, an invertebrate zoologist.*

Dr. Charles E. Herdendorf, one of my former professors at Ohio State and coordinator of our Adjunct Science Program from 1988 to 1995, believes that the rotting wood has created a food chain by providing sustenance to bacteria that serve as the basis of the food chain. To date, 150 species of sea creatures have been cataloged on the shipwreck, and we believe 12 of those to be previously unknown. But it is still not clear how such an isolated site is colonized by such a rich community. We also do not yet know the life expectancy of this mini-ecosystem.

Discovery of the shipwreck has provided scientists and scholars from academic and research institutions throughout the world with new opportunities to explore such questions. More than 100 people have participated in the Adjunct Science Program alone. In addition to deploying experiments directly at the site, they are studying marine specimens, seafloor samples, photographic images, oceanographic data, and historic artifacts recovered by *Nemo*.

The unusual program is possible because the robot was designed to remain on an ocean-floor worksite for 100 hours at a time. This allows the scientific community unparalleled opportunities to study a world heretofore seen only in the brief glimpses afforded by manned submersibles. Consider the implications, for

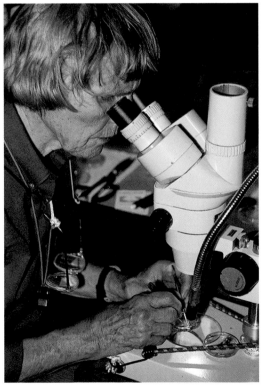

*Dr. Ruth D. Turner of the Museum of Comparative Zoology at Harvard University is an expert in the study of wood-boring bivalves (commonly known as shipworms).*

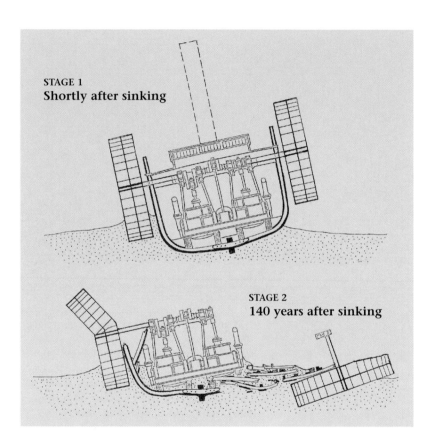

*A 19th-century wood-hulled sidewheeler is shown in two stages of degradation in the deep ocean. The* Central America *is believed to have undergone this type of transformation in the more than 140 years since it sank.*

example, that the majority of pharmaceuticals come from organic materials, and that 80 percent of the earth's biological species may exist in the deep ocean.

One of the scientists responsible for identifying new species at the *Central America* shipwreck is Dr. Henry M. Reiswig of the Redpath Museum and Biology Department at McGill University in Montreal. Dr. Reiswig has learned that 22 different sponge species live on the wreck, including three that were previously unknown. His most significant sponge discovery, however, is the new genus and species *Leioplegma polyphyllon*.

Another expert working with us is Dr. Ruth D. Turner of the Museum of Comparative Zoology at Harvard University, the world's leading authority on wood-boring bivalves. Her studies have revealed that the shipworms infesting the *Central America* are a new species that lives only in the deep ocean. While advancing biological research, work on the *Central America* also provides valuable insight into two developing disciplines: sinking dynamics and degradation mechanics. Sinking dynamics involves studying the precise way a vessel sinks and settles into a particular sea environment and the effect this process has on its structure. As in search theory, sinking dynamics takes into account weather conditions, currents, and sea depth at the time of a sinking, but also considers such factors as the physics of descent and the weight distribution of the ballast.

The ability to analyze the *Central America* in this way enables scientists and engineers to better read sonar signatures, interpret bottom debris, and ultimately learn how to identify the location of other shipwrecks. Understanding how a particular ship in a particular situation is likely to sink—whether it will spin, or drop, or break apart (as did the *Titanic*)—allows us to better determine how, and where, it will land on the bottom, even after a descent of thousands of feet.

Degradation mechanics analyzes the many forces at work on a ship after it reaches the bottom. Shallow-water shipwrecks are far more subject to shifting shoals, weather conditions, and human interference—which often disperse them before they can degrade—while deep-water ship-

*The* Central America *Project's Adjunct Science and Education Program was created in 1988 to study the shipwreck. Participating scientists are examining photographic images, oceanographic data, marine specimens, sea-floor samples, and historic artifacts obtained from the site. Twelve previously unrecorded species of marine animals have been discovered.*

wrecks become victims of organic processes. Before the *Central America* was found, no one knew what sort of havoc the forces of entropy have on a wood-hulled ship in the deep ocean. By studying the degradation process of deep-ocean shipwrecks like the *Central America*, scientists are better able to understand what survives, what decays, and at what rate.

One important offshoot of degradation mechanics is biometallurgy. Dr. Elenora Robbins of the U.S. Geological Survey has been studying the "rusticles," or rust icicles, that hang off the railings, boilers, and other iron fixtures of the sunken sidewheeler. Curiously, these iron growths are combinations of iron oxides, chlorides, and bacteria with the same chemical makeup as those discovered on the *Titanic*. Studies indicate that this curious metal-organic amalgam may have properties that could be used as antitoxins.

The Columbus-America Discovery Group also realized early on that the *Central America* project presents extraordinary educational opportunities. The excitement over a tale of sunken treasure could easily motivate students to learn about related subjects, such as the technology required to recover the treasure, the history of the ship and its passengers, and the scientific discoveries being made at the site. In 1988, team members formed a program designed to reach

*The submersible deploys canisters containing various types of textiles in order to test the effects of submergence in the deep ocean. Nearby, two rows of wood posts have been placed in the mud to attract the wood-boring bivalves believed to be consuming the ship's timbers.*

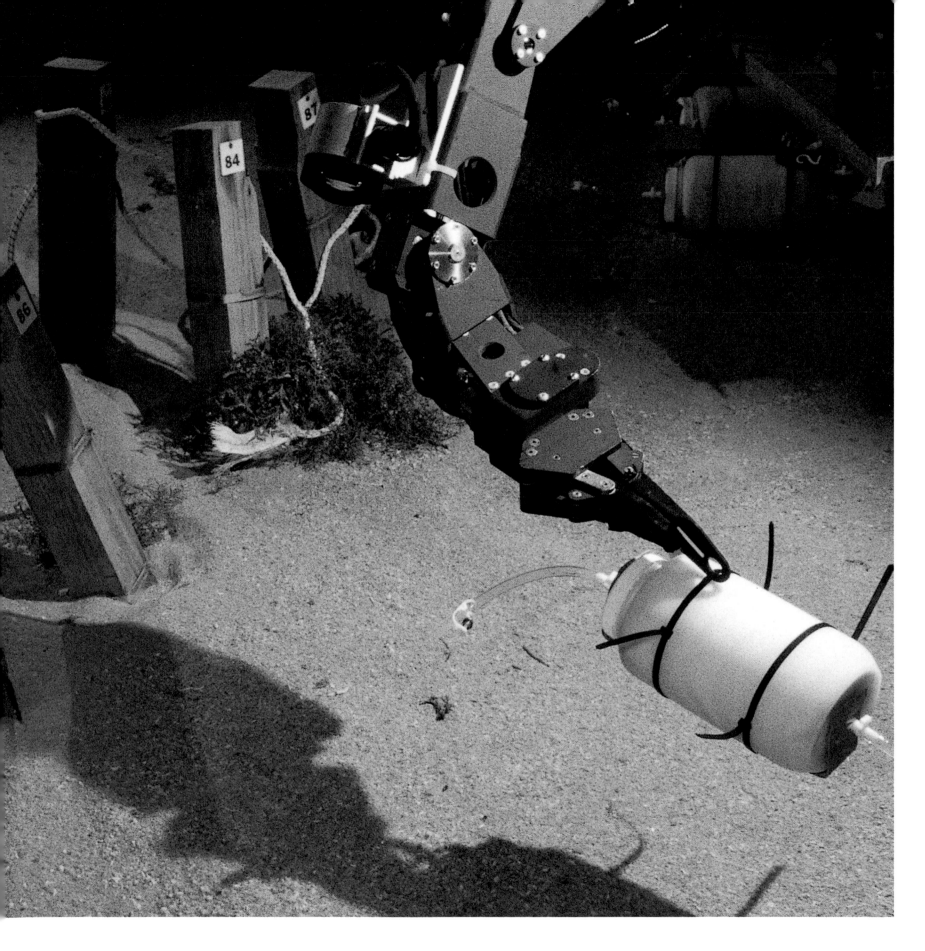

all levels of formal education, from elementary grades through graduate school, and to educate the general public through broadcast media, museum exhibits, popular publications, and public lectures. Since 1989, Columbus-America team members have presented about 800 free programs in schools, civic clubs, university halls, and public auditoriums. Audiences have ranged in age from kindergartners to senior citizens.

Among the highlights of the program is a 1990 project with The Discovery Channel to produce two educational packages for middle-school students—*Investigating History: Treasures from the Deep* and *Investigating Science: Treasures from the Deep*. The packages, which include a laser disc, a computer program, and a classroom guide, have won numerous awards for excellence in educational media and have been used in school systems across the country.

In 1991, the Columbus-America Group worked closely with the Office of Instructional Technology of the South Carolina Department of Education to develop "Project Discovery," a live interactive teleconference for students broadcast over open-circuit educational television channels. Students were able to talk directly with Columbus-America researchers on the *Arctic Discoverer.*

In joint commercial-scientific expeditions, tension can exist between the twin masters of science and business. But on the *Arctic Discoverer* there is an unusual camaraderie between the ship's crew and visiting scientists as they trade off in the control room, seeking gold much of the time and biological and historical specimens, or simply information, the rest. Further opportunities for study are constrained only by technological limitations, and, as the technology improves, the opportunities will rapidly expand, too. This is clearly a rich universe for exploration.

# The Food Chain
## Wood-Borers and Invertebrates

T he sea life calling the *Central America* home makes up a complex food chain, ranging from small animals living off the decaying timbers up to some of the ocean's largest predators. At the chain's base are wood-borers. Commonly known as shipworms, these are actually a type of tiny clam that riddles the wood, boring holes while secreting a hard shell. Infestation with the shallow-water variety would suggest that the *Central America* had not been seaworthy. However, study indicates the clams are actually a newly discovered, deep-ocean variety that appears to have moved in after the ship went down.

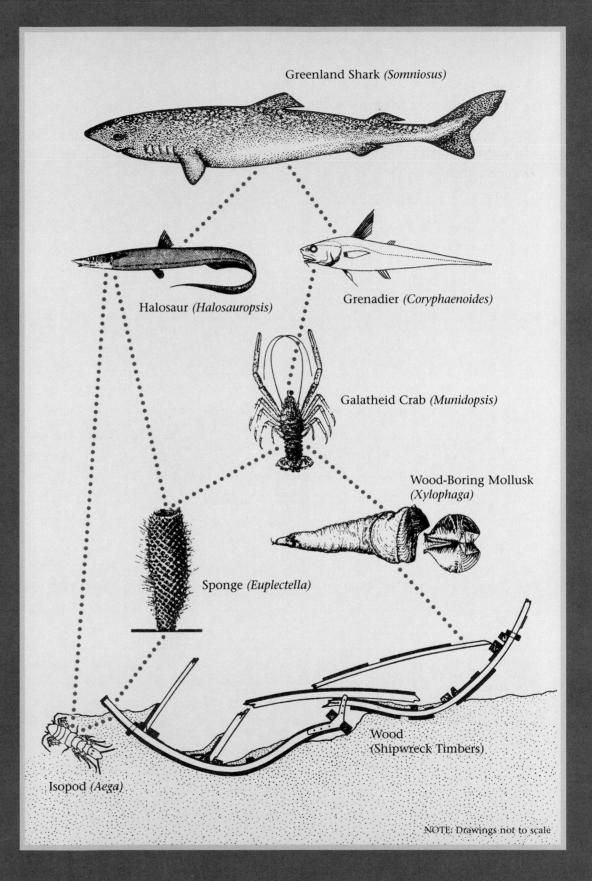

Greenland Shark *(Somniosus)*

Halosaur *(Halosauropsis)*

Grenadier *(Coryphaenoides)*

Galatheid Crab *(Munidopsis)*

Wood-Boring Mollusk *(Xylophaga)*

Sponge *(Euplectella)*

Wood (Shipwreck Timbers)

Isopod *(Aega)*

NOTE: Drawings not to scale

171

## Sessile, or Attached, Invertebrates

Sessile, or attached, invertebrates, such as coral, sea anemones, and sponges, are the next link in the chain and are among the most plentiful of all species at the site. The gold *Chrysogorgia* coral has been seen at shallower depths, but the gold gorgonian coral, which stands erect on metallic-looking stalks attached to pieces of coal (and, ironically, gold), may be a new species altogether. The sea anemones, among the most colorful denizens of the shipwreck, glow brilliant orange—a peculiarity in the

*Hexactinellid sponges colonize timbers of the shipwreck.*

172

lightless depths of the Blake Ridge, where it would seem colors have no use. Attaching themselves to the scattered trunks and other hard objects the shipwreck has left on the sea bottom, they capture their food basket-style instead of with the tentacles used by their shallow-water cousins. The translucent glass sponges, one of 22 sponge species identified on the *Central America* by Dr. Henry Reiswig, have a beautiful, fibrous delicacy. One elaborate specimen is known by the crew as the "Sydney Opera House" for its scalloped white appearance. Interestingly, these creatures

*This undersea specimen has been nicknamed the "Sydney Opera House Sponge" because it resembles its famous namesake in Australia. The delicate sponge might otherwise be appealing to browsing fish, but the tissue contains poisonous chemicals, so it is rarely eaten. Because these emissions may have medicinal value for humans, the sponges are sought for use in research.*

may prove to be the deep ocean's greatest treasure. As sessile invertebrates, they can repel predators only by releasing chemicals. Scientists believe these emissions may contain antiviral, antifungal, and anti-inflammatory agents, as well as agents able to fight cancerous tumors and immune-system diseases. Sponges found at the *Central America* site have been sent to Scripps Oceanographic Institute in San Diego and The Ohio State University for study.

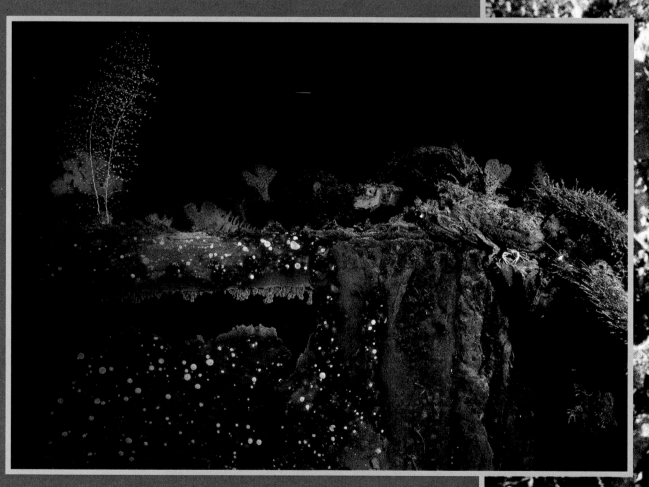

*Above: An anchor chain of the* Central America *drapes over a large iron water tank. Icicle-like rust formations known as "rusticles" can be seen here. Marine animals on top of the tank include golden corals and glass sponges.*

This leather steamer trunk has been colonized by two large, brilliant orange sea anemones and a plumy golden coral. The sea anemones capture their food basket-style.

## Surprise Visitors

Two of the largest animals at the top of the food chain made some very dramatic appearances. Caught on video was a deep-sea octopus with a six-foot arm span; it is thought to be a female and may be an unknown species. She was first seen emerging from her lair deep within the timbers of the ship, and seemed to develop a rapport with the similarly multiarmed *Nemo* as she climbed about the robot's protruding booms and appendages.

Even more breathtaking than the octopus was the 21-foot Greenland shark that swam into *Nemo*'s view during a feeding experiment. When the massive shadow blacking out the monitors began to recede, we realized that the school of swirling eels feeding at the trays had disappeared. (In addition to eels, fish, and seabirds, even reindeer have been found in the stomachs of these cold-water predators.) This Greenland shark was swimming deeper than any shark ever recorded, and 1,000 miles farther south than any other Greenland shark known. The frigid temperature characteristic of the deep ocean may explain its presence.

*This large female octopus, with a six-foot arm spread, is thought to be a new species. It feeds on crabs that crawl over the shipwreck and appears to live in a lair created by the collapsed timbers of the hull. A brittle star can be seen under her leading arm.*

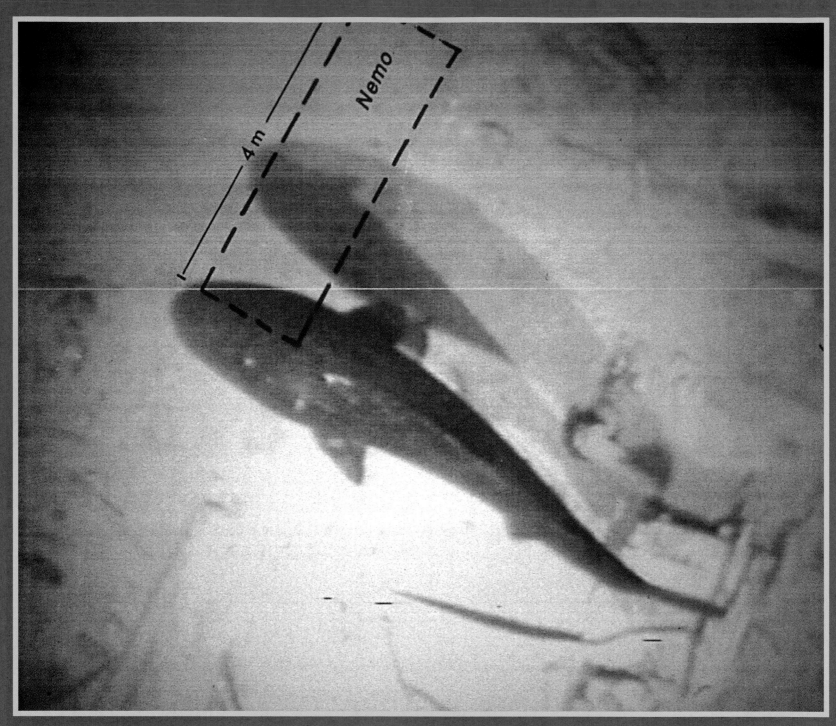

*One of the most startling observations of the expedition came in the early hours of September 1, 1990, when a 21-foot-long Greenland shark cruised past Nemo's cameras. Video transmissions showed it to have a very dark brown skin color and distinctly white and luminous eyes. It was the largest deep-water shark ever seen, and the deepest verified sighting of a large shark (or any shark). The crew likes to say that these attributes make it the largest-deepest shark anybody has ever seen anywhere in the world.*

# Playful Creatures

More mobile than the invertebrates, but no less colorful, are the lively sea crabs and sea stars that scuttle and dart about the shipwreck, as well as the slower-moving sea cucumbers. The galatheid crabs, more commonly known as "squat lobsters," are the ubiquitous little white ghosts of the shipwreck site. Represented by four different species on the ship, they appear everywhere, probing the timbers with their pincers for the wood-boring clams and other small invertebrates they eat.

The deep-sea crab, thought to be another new species because of a unique set of carapace spines, figured in an interesting battle filmed on the site when the bristle worm it was eating was attacked by a blind Ophidion fish. The crab tucked the worm under its carapace and waited until its competitor swam away.

*Five galatheid crabs and two six-armed sea stars were recovered from baited traps set on the shipwreck.*

Among the starfish are brisingids, which include a colony of some 50 brilliantly colored females that live on the *Central America*'s sidewheel. The mating behavior of the brisingid had never before been caught on *Nemo*'s cameras and may be a deep-ocean adaptation. Sea stars, brittle stars, and feather stars, all with different locomotion and feeding methods, also entertained the crew during monotonous hours of work. The light-weight feather stars, named for their feathery bodies, usually crawl or tumble along with the help of the minimal current, but when disturbed by *Nemo*, they were witnessed in the rare act of swimming. Exhibiting a graceful arm-over-arm-over-arm backstroke, the feather star would reach its destination and then parachute in a gentle free fall to a new resting place.

The wormlike sea cucumbers, yet another unrecorded species, are purple or bluish-gray in color and progress over the food-rich wood timbers with a sluglike expansion-and-contraction motion. As they move, they trap small food particles on tiny adhesive pads on ten tentacles. Occasionally, the sea cucumbers were seen ingesting and then spitting out a tiny, indigestible flake of gold.

The Ophidion fish, which were filmed cruising blindly throughout the shipwreck; snubnose eels (during a feeding experiment, these swirled madly around a tray of fishheads after sinking their teeth into the carcasses); and grenadier fish, or rattails, are the voracious eaters of the group. Deep-sea cod hover within three feet of the bottom feeding on crustaceans and small fish, while sluggish, elongated eelpouts curl up in the food trays.

A 14-armed brisingid sea star sits on the port sidewheel of the Central America. The arms of the sea star and a gorgonian coral are being forced to the right by the bottom current, and the rusticle grown on the underside of the sidewheel is bent in the same direction.

*The Central America's rudder stands like a silent sentinel guarding the stern of the shipwreck. In 140 years on the seafloor the wood has been consumed by bacteria and shipworms, leaving only the copper sheathing.*

*I* first met Tommy Thompson when I was chairman of mechanical engineering at The Ohio State University. Tommy was already interested in the marine environment, but Ohio State didn't offer a degree in ocean engineering. I set up a tutorial in which Tommy and I met one-on-one to pursue the deep blue sea and its challenges. How is mankind going to work in the hostile deep-ocean environment? Teaching Tommy was a joy. He was invariably pleasant, intellectually quick, and given to thinking about things both thoroughly and in an unconventional fashion.

*Tommy Thompson and Dr. Glower*

The student-mentor relationship we developed has lasted for years, each of us energizing the other. Tommy frequently returned to discuss his latest projects and to continue our original discussion about the deep ocean. Eventually, Tommy returned to Columbus to work at Battelle Memorial Institute, a think tank, and to continue his research work in deep-ocean engineering. When he approached me about a plan to find and recover a deep-ocean shipwreck, something never done before, I knew he was intellectually prepared to attempt it, and I believed he had the creativity and tenacity to pull it off.

Tommy and I talked about the various aspects of the project. He had decided to recover a shipwreck because he believed it was the best way to begin doing actual work in the deep ocean, going beyond simple photography. In answer to my question about how we were going to work in the deep ocean, he had decided to develop a special robot. Manned submersibles, he reasoned, were too risky and required too much engineering devoted to keeping human beings safe.

It was a pleasure to introduce Tommy to friends who had the financial wherewithal to make the project a reality. They, too, liked Tommy's earnest, businesslike sincerity, his low-key approach, and his extraordinary preparation. The search for the United States Mail Steamship *Central America* would be a viable enterprise.

By the time a student gets to college, he is already a complete person, shaped by his parents, family, teachers, friends, . . . and his DNA, too, probably. I'm thankful to each of those early influences that helped make Tommy such an extraordinary individual. I'm proud to have been his teacher and to have helped him get started on the project that led to man's first working presence in the deep ocean. I value our continuing relationship.

Donald D. Glower, Ph.D.
Former Dean
College of Engineering
The Ohio State University

*I* welcome the opportunity to acknowledge those who have made possible our discovery of *America's Lost Treasure: A Pictorial Chronicle of the Sinking and Recovery of the United States Mail Steamship* Central America—*The Ship of Gold.*

Foremost, we intend this book to honor the 425 men who died when the *Central America* sank and the 153 men, women, and children who survived to tell the tale that guided us to discovering it on the deep-ocean floor. We never have been far from the spirit of those who maintained their courage and determination against a monstrous hurricane, bailed water, hauled coal, and fought the sea for days. These heroes supported one another in body and spirit and rescued the women and children at the cost of their very lives. Their tenacity inspired us in the face of naysayers, modern pirates, false leads, equipment failures, long ordeals at sea away from our families, and interminable legal challenges.

The words of the survivors—who themselves were victims of horrendous suffering before their rescue by less severely damaged ships—guided us to the *Central America*. Through tragic coincidence over a century ago they bequeathed this spectacular treasure to us.

To this day, we take heart from the continued strong support of many descendants of those aboard the *Central America*. We have communicated with them and will keep them informed of future discoveries that may result from our work.

*America's Lost Treasure* is also an opportunity to highlight the work of the scientists and historians around the world who have participated in our expeditions and discovered more than a dozen previously unknown species of sea life. Some of these men and women are searching for new medicines derived from these new species. Others are developing new techniques to conserve artifacts we rescue from the deep ocean. Still others are gaining new knowledge of American history from passenger and ship artifacts. All are advancing our understanding of the deep ocean and how to explore it. These scholars are committed to learning through innovation and continuing discovery. Their boundless spirit of inquiry inspires us.

Finally, I express my gratitude and respect to the men and women who constitute the Columbus-America Discovery Group, and I thank them for their patience throughout a seemingly unending process. I include here three major categories: our financial partners; our technical, shipboard, and support staff; and our families and loved ones.

ACKNOWLEDGMENTS

There would be no Columbus-America Discovery Group without the 161 visionary and adventurous men and women—mostly from landlocked Columbus, Ohio—who invested more than $10 million to sponsor and participate very intensely in deep-ocean discovery. They are an extraordinary group of individuals who remained so helpful, patient, and encouraging during years of work and setbacks that the financing was in fact the least of their contributions. Their gift of faith in me and in our team will remain the most valuable of treasures for us. We dedicate this book to them.

The *Central America* Project represents another invaluable investment, that of the intellectual and physical contribution for many years by scores of highly creative and dedicated historical researchers, engineers, scientists, designers, writers, technicians, the crew of our research ships and planes, logisticians, legal specialists, and office support staff, who literally keep the home office functioning. As a team, they have developed our unique technological capabilities, proficiently operated a wide array of equipment on land and sea, captured on film and video thousands of never-before-seen images, and carefully conducted and documented the recovery of treasure from the *Central America*.

This team created the photographs and researched for years to develop the archival materials used in this publication. They also wrote the manuscript, along with outside consultants, that formed the basis for the book.

Without years of professional help from all of them, there would have been no discovery, no recovery, and no presentation to the world of the treasure of the *Central America*. My respect for them and their diligence continues to grow.

Most important, those of us who have lived this endeavor for years thank our families, loved ones, and friends, both near and extended, who have loved, supported, endured, and nurtured us throughout what started as a search and became a calling. We have drawn our strength from them for years, and always will.

We went to the deep ocean to learn about our past and our future. That discovery will continue.

# CREDITS

Unless otherwise indicated, photographs were provided by Columbus-America Discovery Group, Milt Butterworth, Jr., Director of Photography.

Page 8: Photograph by Henry Groskinsky. Pages 14–15: Reproduced from "A New Map of the United States of America" by J. H. Young, published by Charles DeSilver, Philadelphia. Pages 17, 18, 19: Courtesy of the Bancroft Library, University of California, Berkeley. Pages 20–21: *Yerba Buena, 1847* by Victor Prevost, courtesy of the California Historical Society, San Francisco. Page 22: Courtesy of the California Historical Society, San Marino. Page 23 (above): *California News* by William Sidney Mount, courtesy of The Museums at Stony Brook, Stony Brook, New York; (below): Courtesy of the Huntington Library, San Marino, California. Page 24: *The Steamer Has Arrived*, reproduced from *Hutchings California Magazine*, January 1858. Page 25: Map by Bette Duke; (inset): Reproduced from *Harper's New Monthly Magazine*, March 1858. Pages 26, 27: Lithographs by J. Brandard after drawings by Frank Marryat, courtesy of The New-York Historical Society. Page 28 (top): Painting by J. R. Eyerman, courtesy of the Carl Shaefer Dentzel Collection; (left): Courtesy of the Western History Collection, Denver Public Library. Page 29 (above): Courtesy of the Wells Fargo Bank History Room, San Francisco; (right): *O Boys, I've Struck It Heavy!* by Victor Seaman, courtesy of the Bancroft Library. Pages 30–31: Photographs (composite) by William Shew, courtesy of the Smithsonian Institution, Washington, D.C. Page 31: Courtesy of the Peabody Essex Museum, Salem, Massachusetts. Page 32 (above): Courtesy of the Library of Congress, Washington, D.C.; (below): Photograph by Charles Phillips, courtesy of the Smithsonian Institution. Page 33 (above): Courtesy of the Wells Fargo Bank History Room. Page 34: Reproduced from *Harper's Weekly*, October 24, 1857. Page 35: Reproduced from *Harper's Weekly*, October 10, 1857. Pages 36–37: *Steamship George Law*, courtesy of The Mariners' Museum, Newport News, Virginia. Page 38: Photographs courtesy of Mrs. Alice McCully. Page 39: Courtesy of the Eldredge Collection, The Mariners' Museum. Page 40 (above and below left): Courtesy of Mrs. Patricia Hull Milan and Mrs. Ruth Hull Falk; (above right): Courtesy of Mrs. Genevieve Ellis Gross; (right): Courtesy of the M. H. DeYoung Memorial Museum, San Francisco. Page 41 (left): Reproduced from *Frank Leslie's Illustrated Newspaper*, October 10, 1857; (above): Courtesy of the California Historical Society, San Francisco. Page 42 (above): Reproduction courtesy of the California Historical Society, San Francisco. Page 43: Reproduced from the cover of *Harper's New Monthly Magazine*, January 1859. Page 44: Courtesy of the United States Naval Academy Museum, Annapolis, Maryland. Page 45 (right): Courtesy of the United States Naval Academy Museum; (below): Reproduced from *Frank Leslie's Illustrated Newspaper*, September 11, 1858. Page 47: Map by Bette Duke. Pages 48–49: Ship model constructed by William Ballenger. Page 49 (above): Courtesy of the Webb Institute of Naval Architecture, Glen Cove, New York. Pages 50, 51: Adapted from drawings by Cedric Ridgely-Nevitt, courtesy of the Peabody Essex Museum. Page 52: Courtesy of the National Climatic Data Center. Page 53: Reproduced from *Frank Leslie's Illustrated Newspaper*, October 3, 1857. Page 54 (above): Reproduced from *Our First Century*, by R. M. Devens (Springfield, Mass.: C. A. Nichols & Co., 1876). Page 55: Reproduced from *Frank Leslie's Illustrated Newspaper*, October 3, 1857. Page 56: Published by Oliver Ditson & Co., Boston, circa 1857, courtesy of the Library of Congress. Page 57: Courtesy of the San Mateo County Historical Association, San Mateo, California. Page 58: Reproduced from *Frank Leslie's Illustrated Newspaper*, October 10, 1857. Pages 59, 60: Reproduced from *Frank Leslie's Illustrated Newspaper*, October 3, 1857. Pages 62–63: *The Sinking of the Central America*, lithograph published by J. Childs of Philadelphia, courtesy of the Peabody Essex Museum, Salem, Massachusetts. Pages 64–65 and 66–67: Reproduced from *Frank Leslie's Illustrated Newspaper*, October 3, 1857. Pages 68, 69: Reproduced from *Frank Leslie's Illustrated Newspaper*, October 17, 1857. Page 70 (above): Courtesy of the Stevens Children's Home, Swansea, Massachusetts. Page 71 (top left): Reproduced from *Frank Leslie's Illustrated Newspaper*, October 17, 1857; (top right): Engraving from a photograph by Meade Brothers, reproduced from *Frank Leslie's Illustrated Newspaper*, October 17, 1857; (above): Cup photograph courtesy of the Hearst Mining Building, University of California, Berkeley. Page 72: Reproduced from *Frank Leslie's Illustrated Newspaper*, October 3, 1857. Page 77 (above): Reproduced from *Harper's Weekly*, October 3, 1857; (below): Reproduced from the *New-York Daily Tribune*, October 23, 1857. Page 82 (right): Reproduced from Mariners' Weather Log, summer 1991. Page 110: Photograph by Henry Groskinsky. Pages 116, 119 (above): Reproduced from *Hutchings California Magazine*, October 1856. Page 120: Photograph by Henry Groskinsky. Page 124: Photograph by Henry Groskinsky. Page 125: Reproduced from *Hutchings California Magazine*, October 1856. Page 127 (above left): Reproduced from the 1857 *San Francisco City Directory*. Pages 166, 171: Drawings by Charles E. Herdendorf.

# INDEX

Page numbers in *italics* refer to captions and photographs or illustrations.